My Europe Geography Factbook

A Workbook that encompasses the entire continent of Europe.

By Brandy Champeau

Exploring Expression

ISBN-13. 978-1-954057-06-7

A note about this Factbook

The Europe Geography Factbook is a workbook. While there are a number of YouTube videos listed *(and I encourage you to watch them all)* it is **up to you, the learner**, to complete the pages and build your factbook. This means that while many of the aspects will be similar, your finished product will not necessarily look like your neighbors.

My Europe Geography Factbook will be what **you** make it – a comprehensive keepsake guide created by you as you learn about all of the wonderful countries that make up the continent of Europe.

A note about this Factbook

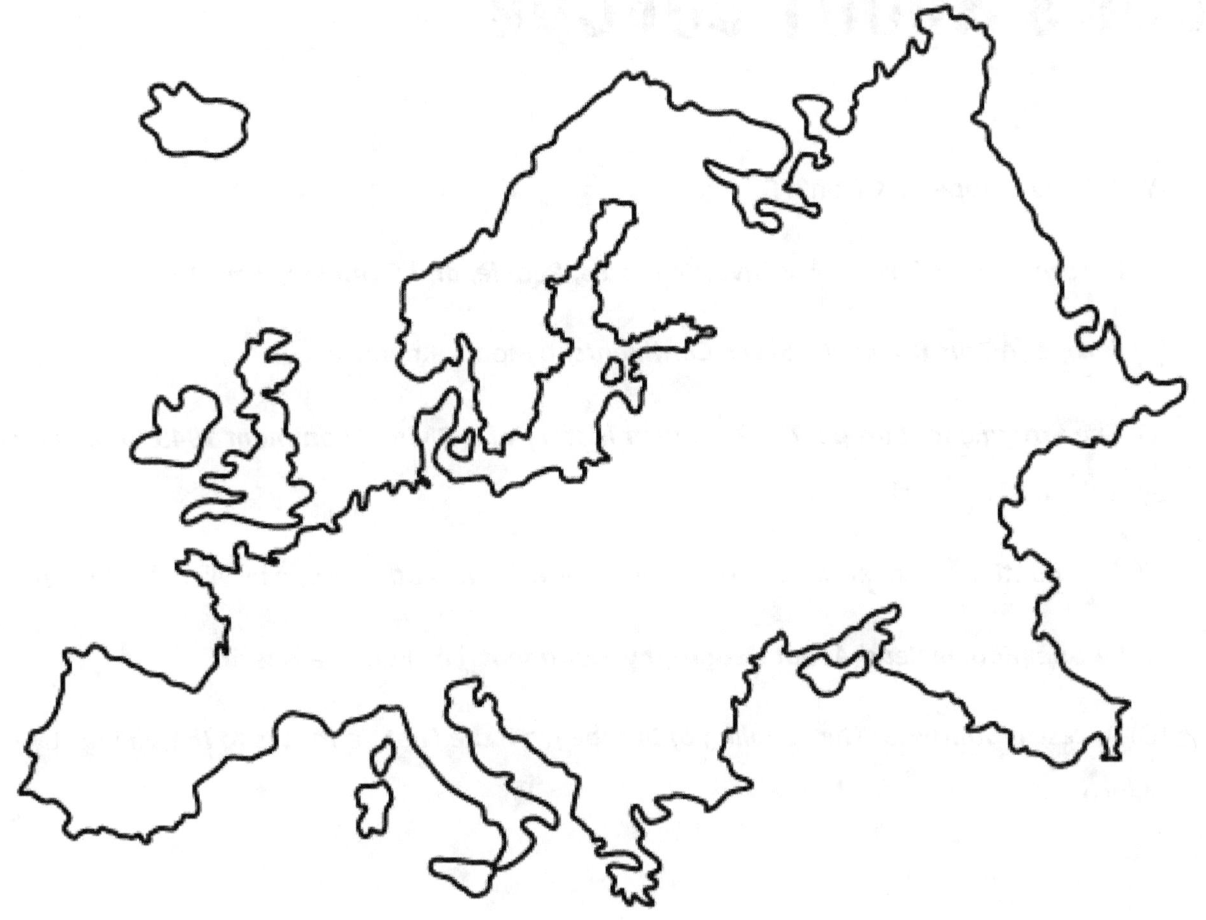

Europe

Books about Europe

1. (Y, O)***Draw Europe*** by Kristin J. Draege
2. (Y) ***For the Love of Europe: My Favorite Places, People, and Stories*** by Rick Steves
3. (Y***) Europe (A True Book: The Seven Continents)*** by Joana Knufinke
4. (O) ***The Struggle for Europe: The Turbulent History of a Divided Continent 1945 to the Present*** by William I. Hitchcock
5. (O) ***Epic Continent: Adventures in the Great Stories that Made Europe*** by Nicholas Jubber
6. (Y) ***Europe (Rookie Read-About Geography: Continents)*** by Rebecca Hirsch
7. (O) ***Ancestral Journeys: The Peopling of Europe from the First Venturers to the Vikings*** by Jean Manco

Games about Europe

1. MAPOMINOES EUROPE – The Ultimate Geography Game
2. Days of Wonder Ticket to Ride: Europe
3. CATAN Histories: Merchants of Europe
4. 10 days in Europe

* (O) books are for older readers; (Y) books are for younger readers

Movies about Europe

1. Mary Poppins (G)(1964)
2. Sword in the Stone (G)(1963)
3. Chronicles of Narnia (PG)(2005)
4. Peter Pan (G)(1953)
5. Willy Wonka and the Chocolate Factory (G)(1971)
6. Robin Hood (G)(1973)
7. Alice in Wonderland (PG)2010)
8. Ratatouille (G)(2007)
9. Beauty and the Beast (PG)(2017)
10. Ben Hur (G)(1959)
11. National Lampoons European Vacation (PG-13)(1985)
12. The Hunchback of Notre Dame (G)(1996)
13. The Sound of Music (G)(1965)
14. Night at the Museum: Secrets of the Tomb (PG)(2014)
15. Harry Potter (PG)(2001)
16. Bend it like Beckham (PG-13)(2002)
17. Brave (PG)(2012)

YouTube videos about Europe General

- The Continent of Europe
  - https://www.youtube.com/watch?v=4c5l1koEnDg
- European Geography Made Easy
  - https://www.youtube.com/watch?v=cJt5Yi48oQ0
- Major Seas & Rivers of Europe Continent
  - https://www.youtube.com/watch?v=NSpK6VkjdP8
- 25 Interesting Facts About Europe That Most People Don't Know
  - https://www.youtube.com/watch?v=3TAjPgFRiaI
- What If Whole European Continent Was Just ONE Country?
  - https://www.youtube.com/watch?v=a_2EbL1ekoU

Continent Fact File: Europe

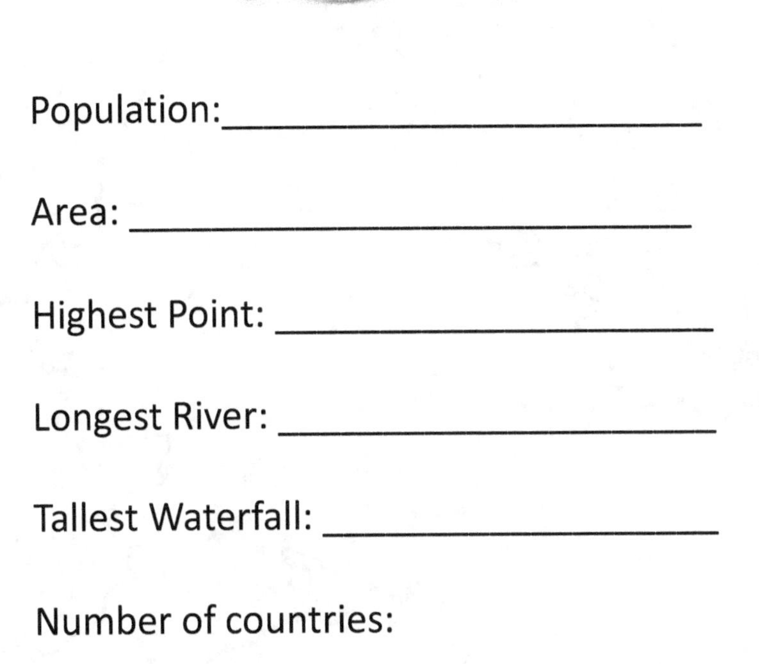

Population:________________________

Area: ________________________

Highest Point: ________________________

Longest River: ________________________

Tallest Waterfall: ________________________

Number of countries:

____

Largest Country: ________________________

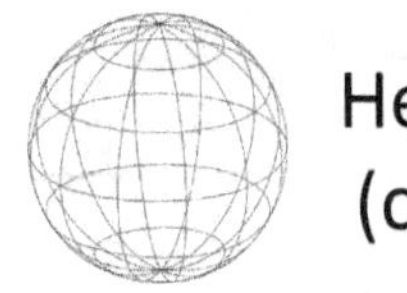

Hemisphere
(circle one)

Northern

Southern

Both

Major
Biomes

1:________________________

2: ________________________

3: ________________________

Other Cool Things about this Continent

1:____

2: ____

3: ____

4: ____

Map it Out: Europe

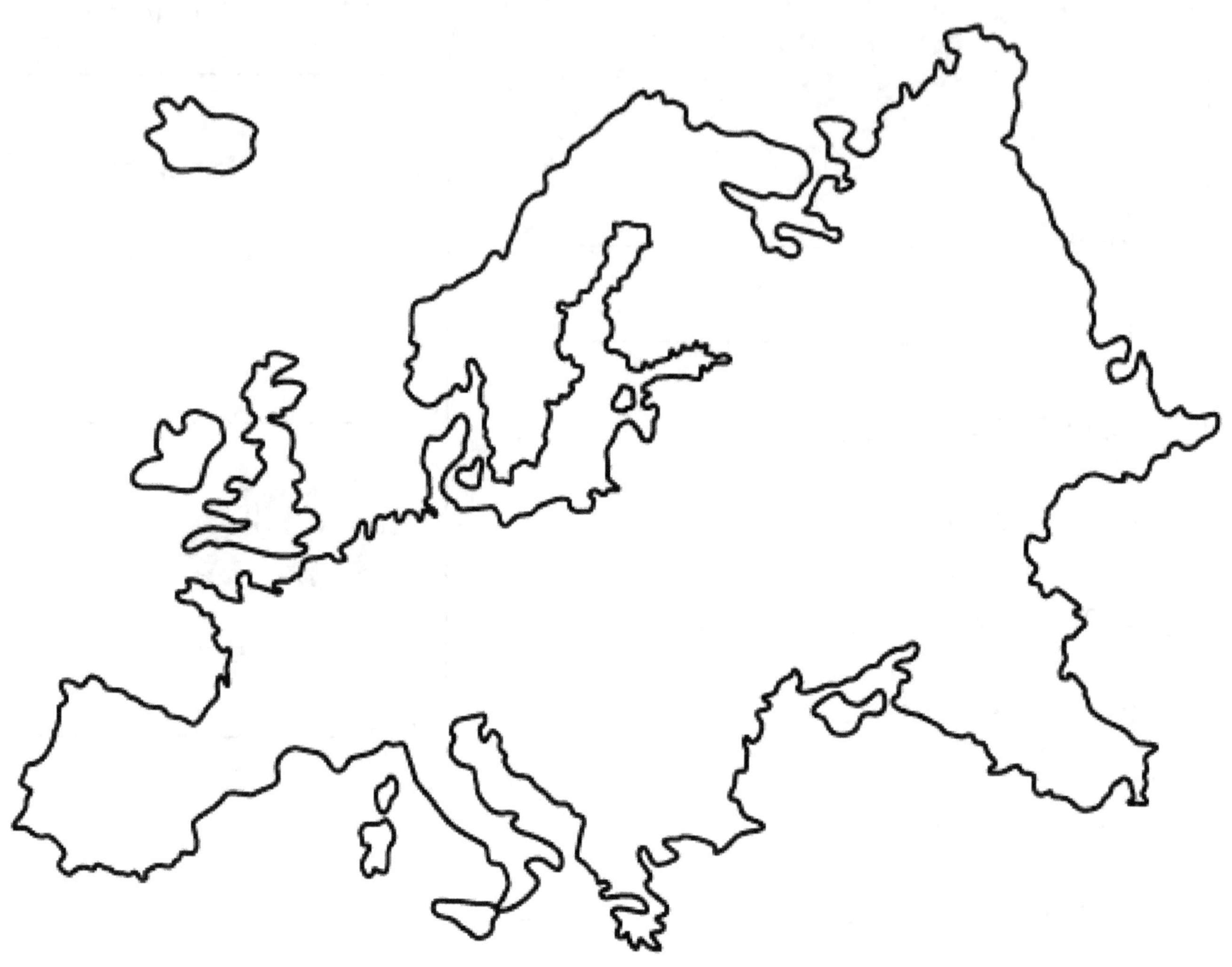

Color and Label the following on the map of Europe:

- ❑ Atlantic Ocean,
- ❑ Mediterranean Sea,
- ❑ Bay of Biscay,
- ❑ North Sea,
- ❑ Baltic Sea,
- ❑ Black Sea
- ❑ Danube river
- ❑ Rhine river
- ❑ Ural mountains
- ❑ Pyrenees
- ❑ The Alps
- ❑ The English Channel
- ❑ The Iberian peninsula

Map it Out: Europe

World Wonders in Europe

7 Wonders of the World

- Wonders of the ancient World
    1. Statue of Zeus at Olympia (Greece)
        1. The Temple of Zeus in Olympia - The Seven Wonders of the Ancient World - See U in History
            1. https://www.youtube.com/watch?v=7lDW7jrDfRY&t=1s
        2. Great Wonders: The Statue of Zeus at Olympia
            1. https://youtube.com/watch?v=9ngny7zfrTU
        3. The Statue of Zeus at Olympia: 7 Ancient Wonders
            1. https://www.youtube.com/watch?v=V0CgaFW1_Rw

    2. Colossus of Rhodes (Greece)
        - The Colossus of Rhodes - 7 Wonders of the Ancient World - See U in History
            - https://www.youtube.com/watch?v=MbFayW5xB9s
        - The Seven Wonders of the Ancient World Episode 2: The Colossus of Rhodes
            - https://www.youtube.com/watch?v=hh-x-KEo4Tg&t=3s
        - The Colossus of Rhodes - Seven Wonders of the Ancient World
            - https://www.youtube.com/watch?v=I99xHsdYlR8

- New wonders of the world

    1. Colosseum (Italy)
        - History of the Roman Colosseum for Kids: All About the Colosseum for Children - FreeSchool
            - https://www.youtube.com/watch?v=e-x74MFiWkg
        - Colosseum - the arena of death
            - https://www.youtube.com/watch?v=ZgRVxJZ8vQU
        - How the Roman Colosseum Was Built
            - https://www.youtube.com/watch?v=09meiYkTsBo
        - What Being a Spectator at the Rome Colosseum Was Like
            - https://www.youtube.com/watch?v=eoi7KzsAUuw

Wonders of the World: Statue of Zeus at Olympia

Draw a Picture of the wonder.

Mark the Location on the Map of Asia

This is a (circle one):	Original Wonder of the World	New Wonder of the World	Wonder of the Natural World

Write a description of the wonder:

Why is it considered a wonder of the world?

Wonders of the World: Colossus of Rhodes

Draw a Picture of the wonder.

Mark the Location on the Map of Asia

This is a (circle one):	Original Wonder of the World	New Wonder of the World	Wonder of the Natural World

Write a description of the wonder:

Why is it considered a wonder of the world?

Wonders of the World: Colosseum

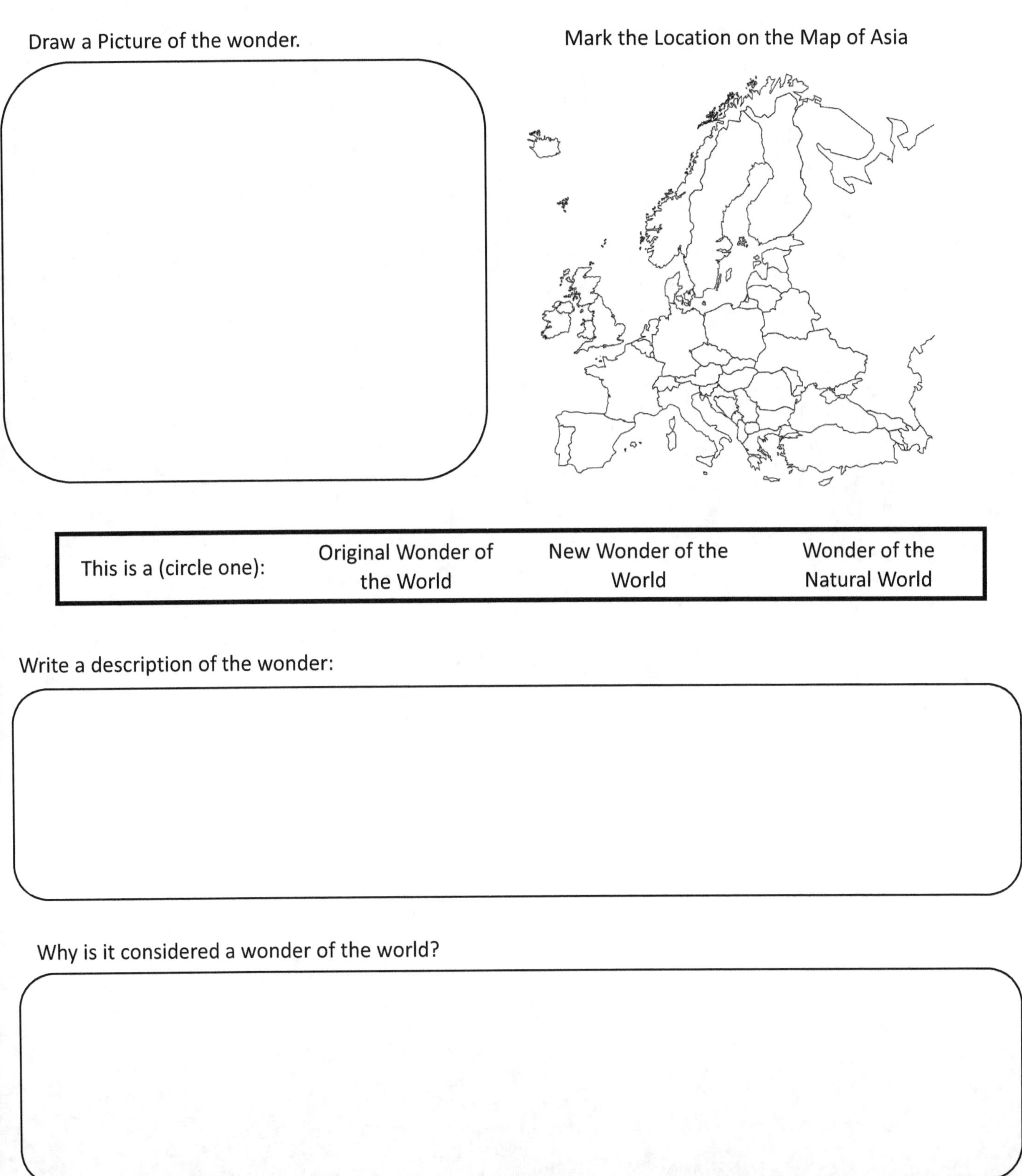

Draw a Picture of the wonder.

Mark the Location on the Map of Asia

This is a (circle one):	Original Wonder of the World	New Wonder of the World	Wonder of the Natural World

Write a description of the wonder:

Why is it considered a wonder of the world?

Countries of Europe

Countries of Europe

1. Albania
2. Andorra
3. Austria
4. Belarus
5. Belgium
6. Bosnia and Herzegovina
7. Bulgaria
8. Croatia
9. Czechia (Czech Republic)
10. Denmark
11. Estonia
12. Finland
13. France
14. Germany
15. Greece
16. Holy See (Vatican)
17. Hungary
18. Iceland
19. Ireland
20. Italy
21. Latvia
22. Liechtenstein
23. Lithuania
24. Luxembourg
25. Malta
26. Moldova
27. Monaco
28. Montenegro
29. Netherlands
30. North Macedonia
31. Norway
32. Poland
33. Portugal
34. Romania
35. Russia
36. San Marino
37. Serbia
38. Slovakia
39. Slovenia
40. Spain
41. Sweden
42. Switzerland
43. Ukraine
44. United Kingdom

Countries of Europe

Albania

- Geography Now! Albania
  - https://www.youtube.com/watch?v=9WZ06pTuqV0
- 15 Facts About Albania
  - https://www.youtube.com/watch?v=LRgy40aF5_U
- Albania Geography/Albania Country Counties
  - https://www.youtube.com/watch?v=_387Pad4psI

Andorra

- Geography Now! Andorra
  - https://www.youtube.com/watch?v=POOvmkhlUD4
- Andorra Geography for Kids
  - https://www.youtube.com/watch?v=GX8Eg5PcuR8
- Andorra: The Micro State at War with Germany for 43 Years
  - https://www.youtube.com/watch?v=T1uNZvZg72o

Austria

- Geography Now! Austria
  - https://www.youtube.com/watch?v=hKsGmyhsKFA
- Austria Geography/Austria Country
  - https://www.youtube.com/watch?v=JmaR4KBRwkY
- AUSTRIA: HISTORY GEOGRAPHY CULTURE FOOD
  - https://www.youtube.com/watch?v=VG1FSnyrcQQ

Belarus

- Geography Now! Belarus
  - https://www.youtube.com/watch?v=nASqSOtXkhk
- Belarus Geography/Belarus Country
  - https://www.youtube.com/watch?v=fjDEAsZ3Tto
- Belarus' Geographic Challenge
  - https://www.youtube.com/watch?v=FfMw-Ngq-Gs
- Belarus. Interesting Facts: Cities People & Nature
  - https://www.youtube.com/watch?v=FBZtUODY2vI

Countries of Europe

Belgium

- Geography Now! Belgium
  - https://www.youtube.com/watch?v=0TuMvWCbM-g
- Belgium Geography/Belgium Country/Belgium
  - https://www.youtube.com/watch?v=udz2W2Jd-6s
- Why does Belgium Exist? (Short Animated Documentary)
  - https://www.youtube.com/watch?v=6eGEX_LTqhQ

Bosnia and Herzegovina

- Geography Now! Bosnia and Herzegovina
  - https://www.youtube.com/watch?v=KO0rEwwyB0g&pbjreload=101
- Why Does Bosnia & Herzegovina Have Two Names?
  - https://www.youtube.com/watch?v=9UuF7f0UPUI
- Bosnia and Herzegovina: an ethnically divided country | DW Documentary
  - https://www.youtube.com/watch?v=lHSO0RQFRe8

Bulgaria

- Geography Now! Bulgaria
  - https://www.youtube.com/watch?v=SlVmp7zBbKU
- Bulgaria
  - https://www.youtube.com/watch?v=0uZ038_15Fc
- A Quick History of Bulgaria
  - https://www.youtube.com/watch?v=3glvDOHPH8o

Croatia

- Geography Now! Croatia
  - https://www.youtube.com/watch?v=Ok5LmqoromI
- Croatia's Geographic Challenge
  - https://www.youtube.com/watch?v=flmB5q6tDDQ
- Croatia Geography
  - https://www.youtube.com/watch?v=74otsAA90sQ
- The Animated History of Croatia
  - https://www.youtube.com/watch?v=TABlbP-tTkk

Countries of Europe

Czechia (Czech Republic)

- Geography Now! Czech Republic (Czechia)
  - https://www.youtube.com/watch?v=-kaF6SnSEo8
- Flag Friday! CZECH REPUBLIC! (CZECHIA)
  - https://www.youtube.com/watch?v=n7QdS-W_HYU
- A Super Quick History of the Czech Republic
  - https://www.youtube.com/watch?v=0fXqkiL_4UM

Denmark

- Geography Now! Denmark
  - https://www.youtube.com/watch?v=Hp0-YP3lADk
- 10 + Surprising Facts About Denmark
  - https://www.youtube.com/watch?v=87dtLCm8e3k
- Denmark Song | Learn Facts about Denmark the Musical Way
  - https://www.youtube.com/watch?v=h-W_kjs-9Ys

Estonia

- Geography Now! Estonia
  - https://www.youtube.com/watch?v=1TTPq38LyPU
- Flag Friday! ESTONIA (Geography Now!)
  - https://www.youtube.com/watch?v=FskySq7GPEA
- Estonia | Geography and History
  - https://www.youtube.com/watch?v=5I205c9phKA
- 10+ Amazing Facts About Estonia
  - https://www.youtube.com/watch?v=7_FNi4L5qLM

Finland

- Geography Now! Finland
  - https://www.youtube.com/watch?v=DxxZOsfsIUM
- The Animated History of Finland
  - https://www.youtube.com/watch?v=TcXXJis03SE
- Nature, geography and history of Finland
  - https://www.youtube.com/watch?v=fx97_nrwD1Y

Countries of Europe

France

- Why France's Geography is Almost Perfect
    - https://www.youtube.com/watch?v=2iQFNtHnpnQ
- Geography Now! France
    - https://www.youtube.com/watch?v=g0QrBphsioM
- The Animated History of France
    - https://www.youtube.com/watch?v=ZNk2QOn9oGE

Germany

- Geography Now! Germany
    - https://www.youtube.com/watch?v=wuClZjOdT30
- Flag Friday! Germany Geography Now!
    - https://www.youtube.com/watch?v=WHd28MTV4cE
- Focus on Germany! Country Profile and Geographical Info
    - https://www.youtube.com/watch?v=YyYuht9cYXY

Greece

- Geography Now! Greece
    - https://www.youtube.com/watch?v=Cp3yabqF4Uw
- Interesting facts about the geography of ancient Greece story for kids
    - https://www.youtube.com/watch?v=dE_VxVQ8cCA
- Flag Friday Greece! (Geography Now)
    - https://www.youtube.com/watch?v=cwJ4gdcArmg

Holy See (Vatican)

- Vatican City Explained
    - https://www.youtube.com/watch?v=OPHRIjI3hXs
- Focus on Vatican City! Geographical Info and Country Profile
    - https://www.youtube.com/watch?v=3AZcNJkvCsQ
- What Is Life Like In The Smallest Country In The World?
    - https://www.youtube.com/watch?v=Yk_oxoDmgxs

Countries of Europe

Hungary

- Geography Now! Hungary (ft. Nick Uhas/ Nickipedia)
  - https://www.youtube.com/watch?v=omx66rFK5yM
- Flag/ Fan Friday HUNGARY (Geography Now!)
  - https://www.youtube.com/watch?v=GwWCepOCn-g
- Introducing Hungary
  - https://www.youtube.com/watch?v=YLZV3hbSLos

Iceland

- Geography Now! Iceland
  - https://www.youtube.com/watch?v=ocE9DNZxPUk
- Iceland's Volcanic World | National Geographic
  - https://www.youtube.com/watch?v=tUaN_tki82o
- The Animated History of Iceland
  - https://www.youtube.com/watch?v=JzYvFypr26U

Ireland

- Geography Now! Ireland
  - https://www.youtube.com/watch?v=yWZiO7YNoPQ
- Destination Ireland | National Geographic
  - https://www.youtube.com/watch?v=bQwdahZwe0M
- Flag/Fan Friday IRELAND Geography Now!
  - https://www.youtube.com/watch?v=HpIPtsWH4KU

Italy

- Geography Now! Italy
  - https://www.youtube.com/watch?v=G_KMyblvv4c
- Flag / Fan Friday ITALY! (Geography Now)
  - https://www.youtube.com/watch?v=jo6-0q90DZs
- Italy Song | Learn Facts About Italy the Musical Way
  - https://www.youtube.com/watch?v=v5MIBsZv19U

Countries of Europe

Latvia

- Geography Now! Latvia
    - https://www.youtube.com/watch?v=3_kocBCsIbk
- Flag/ Fan Friday LATVIA (Geography Now!)
    - https://www.youtube.com/watch?v=J6lyU-n8JbE
- The History of Latvia
    - https://www.youtube.com/watch?v=MIp_udoTgiQ

Liechtenstein

- Geography Now! LIECHTENSTEIN
    - https://www.youtube.com/watch?v=rTiLTnWM7vQ
- Liechtenstein: Europe's Last Absolute Monarchy
    - https://www.youtube.com/watch?v=BZ9CPEM_zw0
- Focus on Liechtenstein! Country Profile and Geographical Info
    - https://www.youtube.com/watch?v=4rYTkJnACJw

Lithuania

- Geography Now! Lithuania
    - https://www.youtube.com/watch?v=9Yxwjy4pvsM
- FLAG / FAN FRIDAY LITHUANIA! (Geography Now!)
    - https://www.youtube.com/watch?v=r6IF967vlqg
- What is LITHUANIA? (My Country You Know Nothing About)
    - https://www.youtube.com/watch?v=WH9mTk1mxkI

Luxembourg

- Geography Now! LUXEMBOURG
    - https://www.youtube.com/watch?v=Bw8g_1VEEL8
- Facts about a really small country: Luxembourg
    - https://www.youtube.com/watch?v=PXkZVFZsbug
- Why Does Luxembourg Exist? (Short Animated Documentary)
    - https://www.youtube.com/watch?v=c7I8kdzH2LA

Countries of Europe

Malta

- Geography Now! MALTA
    - https://www.youtube.com/watch?v=Qee_dxMvids
- Malta, small country - great history
    - https://www.youtube.com/watch?v=ozdEOGYaWJc
- Europe's tiny paradise: Facts about Malta
    - https://www.youtube.com/watch?v=g6RQrJu3uC8

Moldova

- Geography Now! MOLDOVA
    - https://www.youtube.com/watch?v=cARe_1cRj6E
- MOLDOVA is an Interesting Place
    - https://www.youtube.com/watch?v=TsLUgtE3828
- Flag/ Fan Friday! MOLDOVA Geography Now!
    - https://www.youtube.com/watch?v=zxXoMs30kZg

Monaco

- Geography Now! MONACO
    - https://www.youtube.com/watch?v=gZ38gYvhiZA
- Flag/ Fan Friday MONACO (Geography Now!)
    - https://www.youtube.com/watch?v=Hqs6Rzndelo
- Monaco - The Richest Country in the World
    - https://www.youtube.com/watch?v=EzNHVH3f9Tk

Montenegro

- Geography Now! MONTENEGRO
    - https://www.youtube.com/watch?v=uBjUOtlnm5Y
- How did Montenegro Become Independent (Again)? | From Kingdom to Republic via 5 Countries!
    - https://www.youtube.com/watch?v=StLrswQMtro
- History Of Montenegro
    - https://www.youtube.com/watch?v=PSd4IjcnU9o

Countries of Europe

Netherlands

- Geography Now! NETHERLANDS
  - https://www.youtube.com/watch?v=f4TmQEZzsec&t=34s
- Holland's Barriers to The Sea
  - https://www.youtube.com/watch?v=aUqrBV4SiqQ
- Holland vs the Netherlands
  - https://www.youtube.com/watch?v=eE_IUPInEuc

North Macedonia

- Geography Now! Rep. of North Macedonia
  - https://www.youtube.com/watch?v=hoBQRhNbreI
- Flag/ Fan Friday Rep. of North Macedonia (Geography Now!)
  - https://www.youtube.com/watch?v=DAIyRVxrjP4
- BBC Travel Show - Macedonia (Week 35)
  - https://www.youtube.com/watch?v=6yDF3CB078I

Norway

- Geography Now! NORWAY
  - https://www.youtube.com/watch?v=bAGhXcYc0o4
- Norway - The land of fjords
  - https://www.youtube.com/watch?v=Zcx3CDGLwkk
- NORWAY (Documentary, Discovery, History)
  - https://www.youtube.com/watch?v=B25DbSNoyRs

Poland

- Geography Now! POLAND (ft. Art Napiontek & Commonwealth Realm)
  - https://www.youtube.com/watch?v=Hn8XXPl1vjU
- Why Poland's Geography is the Worst
  - https://www.youtube.com/watch?v=jZ6EHGTVr9w
- 10 + Interesting Facts About Poland
  - https://www.youtube.com/watch?v=oKLFuhRej3o

Countries of Europe

Portugal

- Geography Now! PORTUGAL
    - https://www.youtube.com/watch?v=mq6L8CnNJXc&t=724s
- Flag/ Fan Friday PORTUGAL (Geography Now!)
    - https://www.youtube.com/watch?v=ZI0hsvU17h4&t=264s
- Why wasn't Portugal conquered by Spain?
    - https://www.youtube.com/watch?v=EFvsIhX2iog

Romania

- Geography Now! ROMANIA
    - https://www.youtube.com/watch?v=ZRMbh0wSly0
- Geopolitics of Romania
    - https://www.youtube.com/watch?v=7j5B_ADq9RY
- The history of Romania explained in 10 minutes
    - https://www.youtube.com/watch?v=Vxsm2K7CxNU

Russia

- Geography Now! RUSSIA
    - https://www.youtube.com/watch?v=K8zAbdYx9SU&t=1476s
- Russia's Geography Problem
    - https://www.youtube.com/watch?v=v3C_5bsdQWg
- Russia. Interesting Facts About Russia.
    - https://www.youtube.com/watch?v=mORJmK1Ljgk

San Marino

- Geography Now! SAN MARINO
    - https://www.youtube.com/watch?v=SU4W_tIFbTc&t=679s
- Why wasn't San Marino annexed by Italy?
    - https://www.youtube.com/watch?v=mDbG7UjRP_w
- San Marino: The Oldest Republic in the World
    - https://www.youtube.com/watch?v=gDEpnWjHouk

Countries of Europe

Serbia

- Geography Now! SERBIA!
  - https://www.youtube.com/watch?v=1pxrIj9Xyps
- Serbia | Geography Rush | Everything About Serbia
  - https://www.youtube.com/watch?v=vi5wCJT6sJ0
- 10 + Surprising Facts About Serbia
  - https://www.youtube.com/watch?v=LkUyOUvai50

Slovakia

- Slovakia | Geography and History
  - https://www.youtube.com/watch?v=qm1sSkJkUZ4
- History of Slovakia
  - https://www.youtube.com/watch?v=F8H5leO91R0
- 7 Facts about Slovakia
  - https://www.youtube.com/watch?v=BNWFg14yVNU

Slovenia

- The Waters of Slovenia | National Geographic
  - https://www.youtube.com/watch?v=RpG8vuvqDbc
- 10+ Surprising Facts About Slovenia
  - https://www.youtube.com/watch?v=kmYS5rFO95k
- The Best of Slovenia
  - https://www.youtube.com/watch?v=I8DlXa_933Y

Spain

- Destination Spain | National Geographic
  - https://www.youtube.com/watch?v=oyXNducx4QQ
- The Animated History of Spain
  - https://www.youtube.com/watch?v=nPcfZLaMoAo
- Spain Song | Learn Facts About Spain the Musical Way
  - https://www.youtube.com/watch?v=WuI8ACL_W_8

Countries of Europe

Sweden

- Zooming in on SWEDEN | Geography of Sweden with Google Earth
    - https://www.youtube.com/watch?v=sz__5kSIB3Y
- Geopolitics of Sweden
    - https://www.youtube.com/watch?v=GQT4unko248
- The Economy of Sweden
    - https://www.youtube.com/watch?v=2E0dWHCnic8

Switzerland

- Zooming in on SWITZERLAND | Geography of Switzerland with Google Earth
    - https://www.youtube.com/watch?v=XVvzE5bLfwA
- Everything You Need to Know About Switzerland
    - https://www.youtube.com/watch?v=ShWBUWyD3AA
- The Animated History of Switzerland
    - https://www.youtube.com/watch?v=snFjkU85EqI

Ukraine

- Zooming in on Ukraine | Geography of Ukraine with Google Earth
    - https://www.youtube.com/watch?v=zDGA-iLvmNA
- The Animated History of Ukraine
    - https://www.youtube.com/watch?v=zJvz3Ai9Ppw
- 10 FACTS ABOUT UKRAINE | GoFacts
    - https://www.youtube.com/watch?v=tAS1lcwrggE

United Kingdom

- The Difference between the United Kingdom, Great Britain and England Explained
    - https://www.youtube.com/watch?v=rNu8XDBSn10
- Zooming in on UK | Geography of UK with Google Earth
    - https://www.youtube.com/watch?v=AjtOmNc-SNc
- United Kingdom UK - History and Geography in 4 minutes - mini history - mini geography
    - https://www.youtube.com/watch?v=ZQIX9OP59ng

Albania

Color the country's flag in the box above.

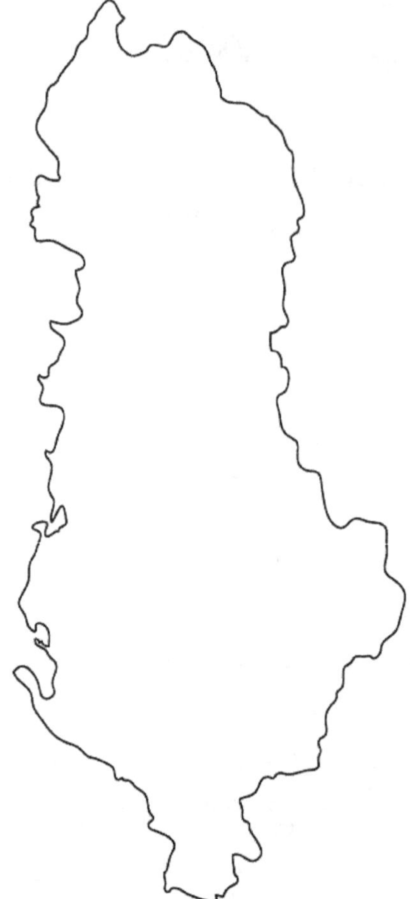

Label the capital city and any major physical features such as mountains, rivers, oceans or seas **in or around** this country.

Country Name: Albania

Population: ______________________

Area: ______________________

Type of Government: ______________

Capital City: ______________________

Religion(s): ______________________

Language(s): ______________________

Currency: ______________________

Climate: ______________________

Time Zone: ______________________

Major Exports

1: ______________________

2: ______________________

3: ______________________

Mountains, Rivers and Lakes

1: ______________________

2: ______________________

3: ______________________

Other Cool Things about this Country

1: ____

2: ____

3: ____

4: ____

Andorra

Color the country's flag in the box above.

Label the capital city and any major physical features such as mountains, rivers, oceans or seas **in or around** this country.

Country Name: Andorra

Population:____________________

Area: ____________________

Type of Government: ____________

Capital City: ____________________

Religion(s): ____________________

Language(s): ____________________

Currency: ____________________

Climate: ____________________

Time Zone: ____________________

Major Exports

1:________________

2: ________________

3: ________________

Mountains, Rivers and Lakes

1:________________

2: ________________

3: ________________

Other Cool Things about this Country

1:____

2: ____

3: ____

4: ____

Austria

Color the country's flag in the box above.

Label the capital city and any major physical features such as mountains, rivers, oceans or seas **in or around** this country.

Country Name: Austria

Population:__________________________

Area: ______________________________

Type of Government: ________________

Capital City: _________________________

Religion(s): __________________________

Language(s): _________________________

Currency: ___________________________

Climate: _____________________________

Time Zone: __________________________

Major Exports

1:_____________________

2: _____________________

3: _____________________

Mountains, Rivers and Lakes

1:_______________________

2: ______________________

3: ______________________

Other Cool Things about this Country

1:____

2: ____

3: ____

4: ____

Belarus

Color the country's flag in the box above.

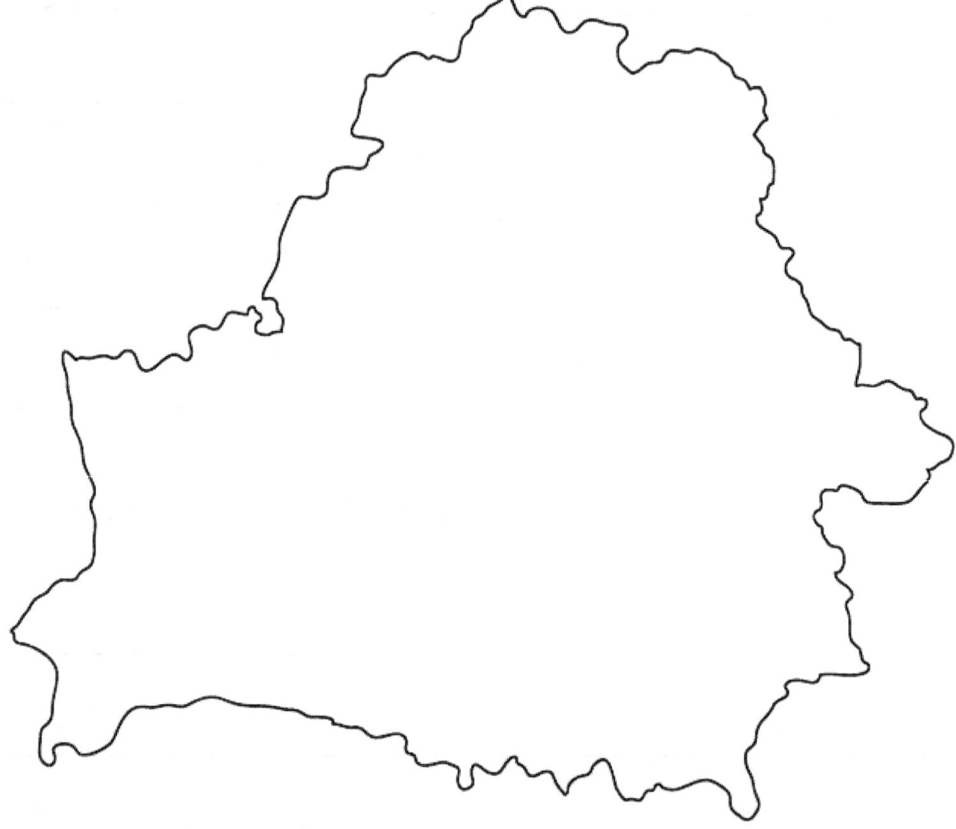

Label the capital city and any major physical features such as mountains, rivers, oceans or seas **in or around** this country.

Country Name: Belarus

Population:____________________________

Area: _______________________________

Type of Government: ________________

Capital City: __________________________

Religion(s): ___________________________

Language(s): __________________________

Currency: ____________________________

Climate: _____________________________

Time Zone: ___________________________

Major Exports

1:______________________

2: ______________________

3: ______________________

Mountains, Rivers and Lakes

1:________________________

2: _______________________

3: _______________________

Other Cool Things about this Country

1:____

2: ____

3: ____

4: ____

Belgium

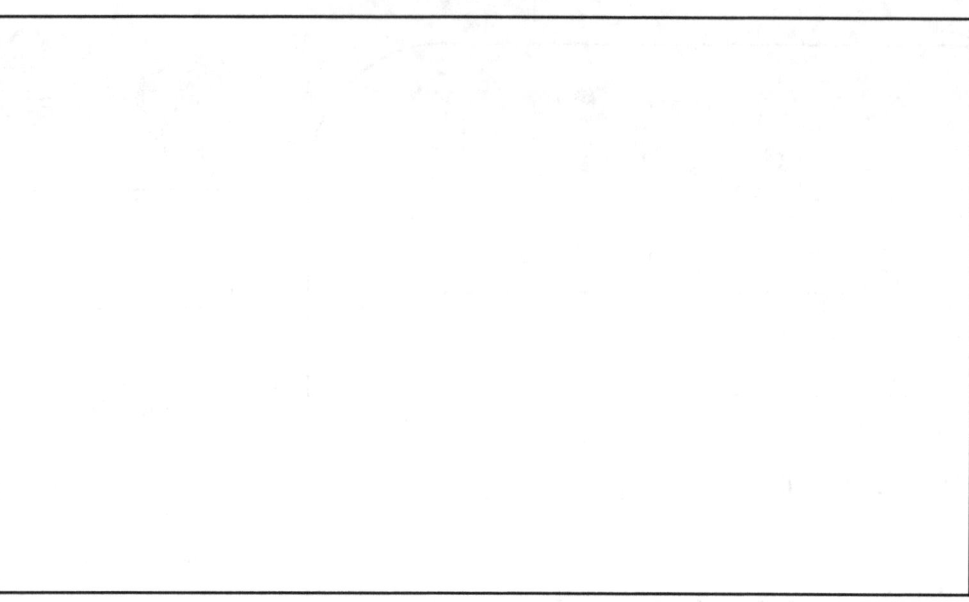

Color the country's flag in the box above.

Label the capital city and any major physical features such as mountains, rivers, oceans or seas **in or around** this country.

Country Name: Belgium

Population: ____________________________

Area: ________________________________

Type of Government: _________________

Capital City: ___________________________

Religion(s): ____________________________

Language(s): ___________________________

Currency: ______________________________

Climate: _______________________________

Time Zone: ____________________________

Major Exports

1: _______________________

2: _______________________

3: _______________________

Mountains, Rivers and Lakes

1: _______________________

2: _______________________

3: _______________________

Other Cool Things about this Country

1: ____

2: ____

3: ____

4: ____

Bosnia and Herzegovinia

Color the country's flag in the box above.

Label the capital city and any major physical features such as mountains, rivers, oceans or seas **in or around** this country.

Country Name: Bosnia and Herzegovina

Population:____________________

Area: ____________________

Type of Government: ____________________

Capital City: ____________________

Religion(s): ____________________

Language(s): ____________________

Currency: ____________________

Climate: ____________________

Time Zone: ____________________

Major Exports

1:____________________

2: ____________________

3: ____________________

Mountains, Rivers and Lakes

1:____________________

2: ____________________

3: ____________________

Other Cool Things about this Country

1:____

2: ____

3: ____

4: ____

Bulgaria

Color the country's flag in the box above.

Label the capital city and any major physical features such as mountains, rivers, oceans or seas **in or around** this country.

Country Name: Bulgaria

Population:__________________________

Area: ______________________________

Type of Government: ________________

Capital City: _________________________

Religion(s): __________________________

Language(s): _________________________

Currency: ___________________________

Climate: ____________________________

Time Zone: __________________________

Major Exports

1:_____________________

2: _____________________

3: _____________________

Mountains, Rivers and Lakes

1:_______________________

2: ______________________

3: ______________________

Other Cool Things about this Country

1:____

2: ____

3: ____

4: ____

Croatia

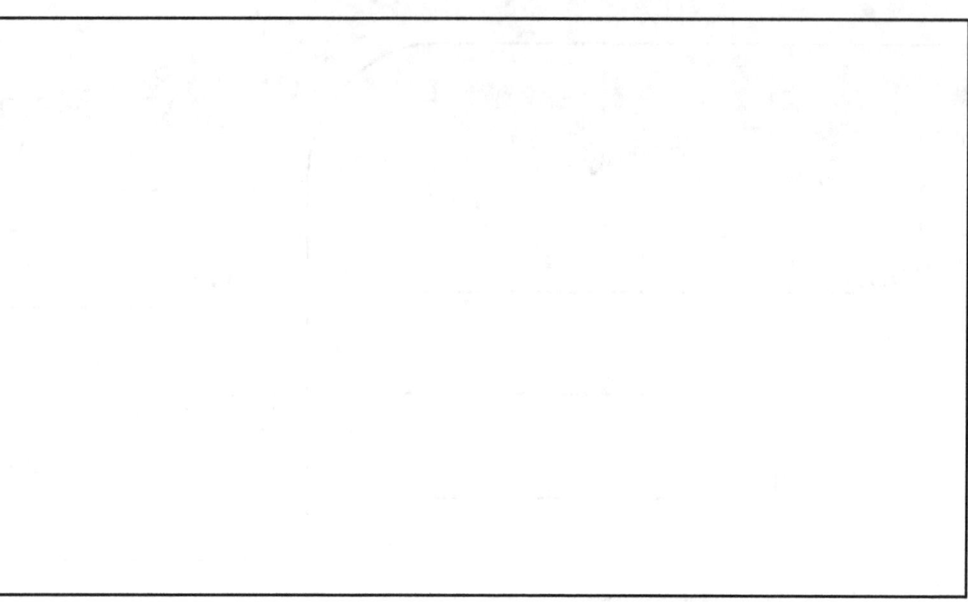

Color the country's flag in the box above.

Label the capital city and any major physical features such as mountains, rivers, oceans or seas **in or around** this country.

Country Name: Croatia

Population: ______________________

Area: ______________________

Type of Government: ______________

Capital City: ______________________

Religion(s): ______________________

Language(s): ______________________

Currency: ______________________

Climate: ______________________

Time Zone: ______________________

Major Exports

1: ______________________

2: ______________________

3: ______________________

Mountains, Rivers and Lakes

1: ______________________

2: ______________________

3: ______________________

Other Cool Things about this Country

1: ____

2: ____

3: ____

4: ____

Czechia (Czech Republic)

Color the country's flag in the box above.

Label the capital city and any major physical features such as mountains, rivers, oceans or seas **in or around** this country.

Country Name: Czechia (Czech Republic)

Population: ____________________

Area: ____________________

Type of Government: ____________________

Capital City: ____________________

Religion(s): ____________________

Language(s): ____________________

Currency: ____________________

Climate: ____________________

Time Zone: ____________________

Major Exports

1: ____________________

2: ____________________

3: ____________________

Mountains, Rivers and Lakes

1: ____________________

2: ____________________

3: ____________________

Other Cool Things about this Country

1: ____________________

2: ____________________

3: ____________________

4: ____________________

Denmark

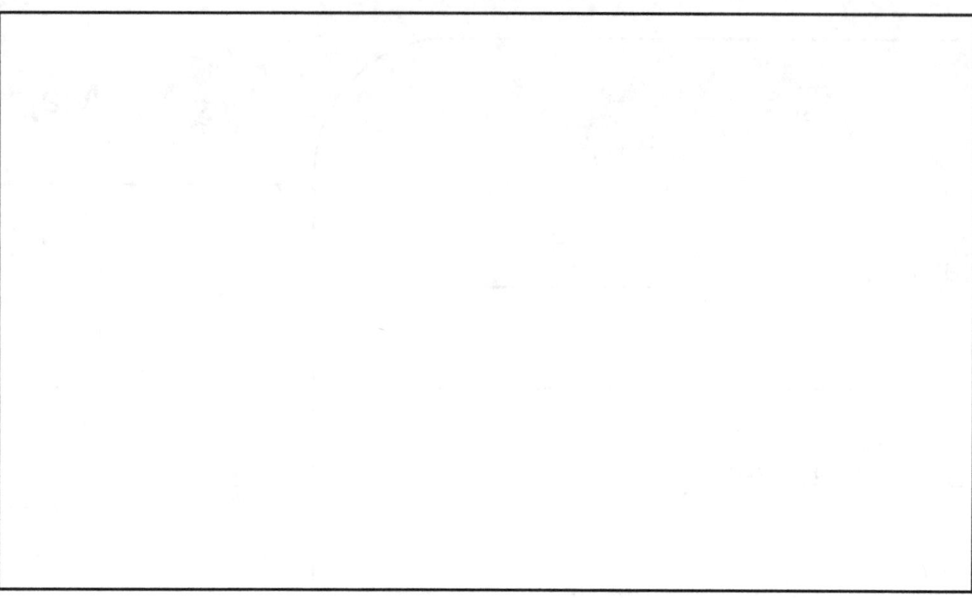

Color the country's flag in the box above.

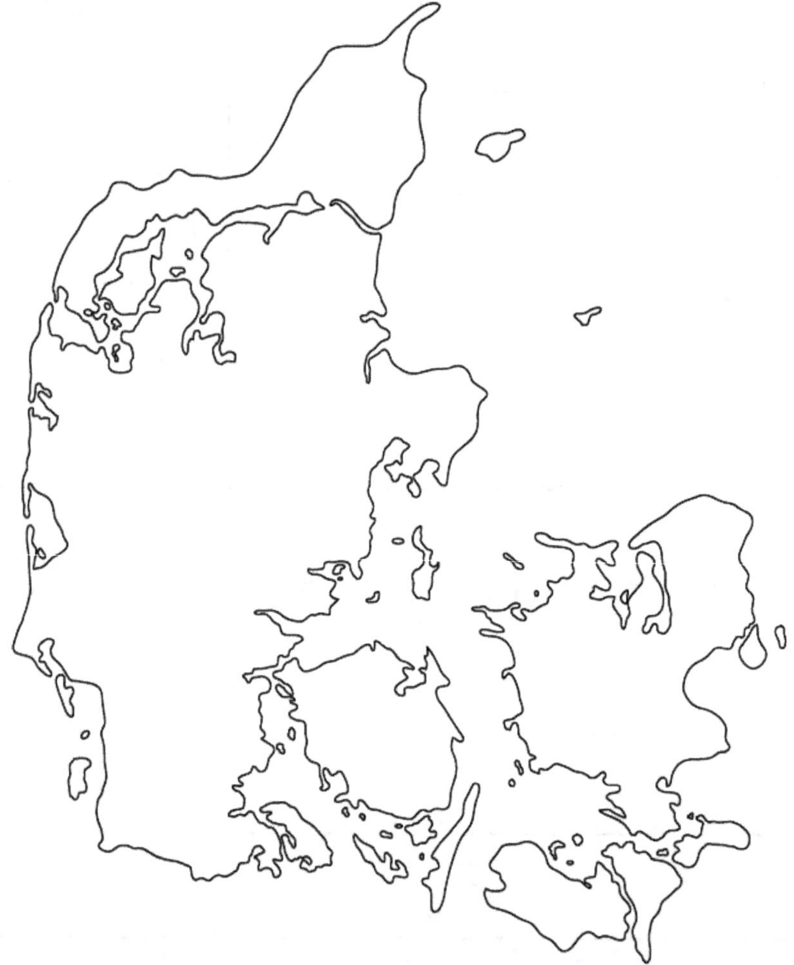

Label the capital city and any major physical features such as mountains, rivers, oceans or seas **in or around** this country.

Country Name: Denmark

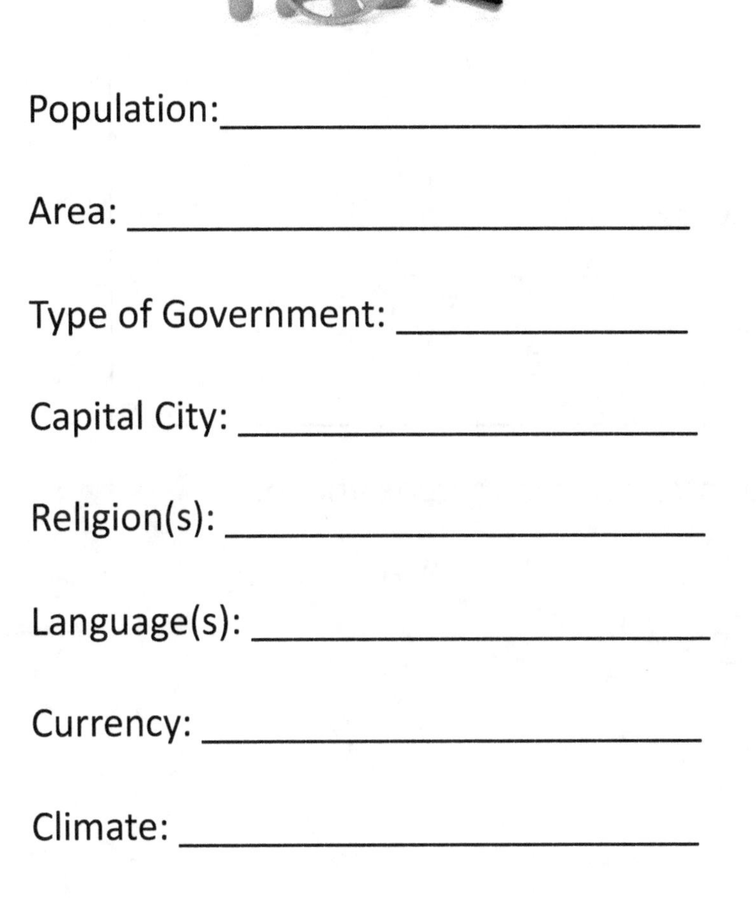

Population:________________________

Area: ________________________

Type of Government: _______________

Capital City: ________________________

Religion(s): ________________________

Language(s): ________________________

Currency: ________________________

Climate: ________________________

Time Zone: ________________________

Major Exports

1:____________________

2: ____________________

3: ____________________

Mountains, Rivers and Lakes

1:____________________

2: ____________________

3: ____________________

Other Cool Things about this Country

1:____

2: ____

3: ____

4: ____

Estonia

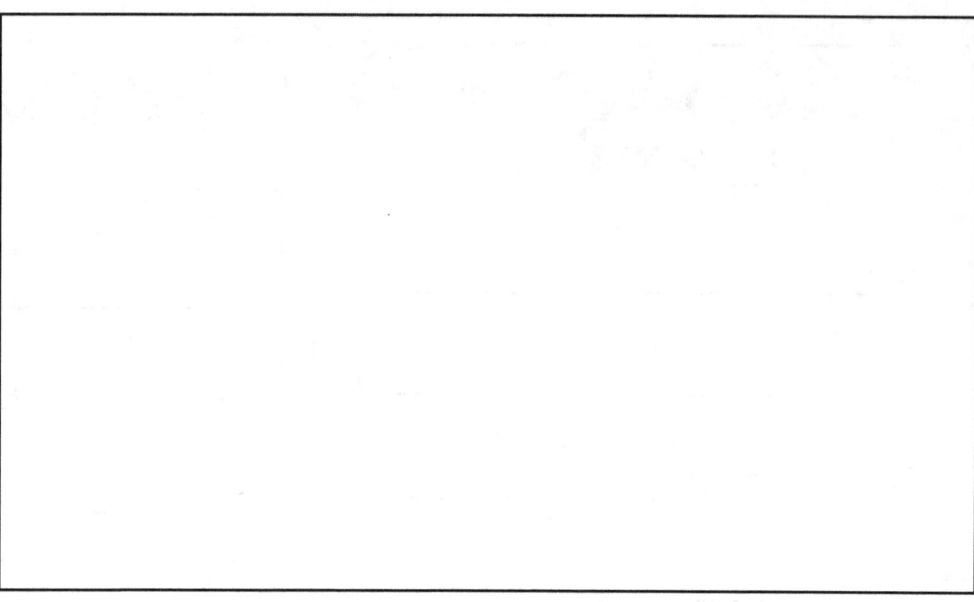

Color the country's flag in the box above.

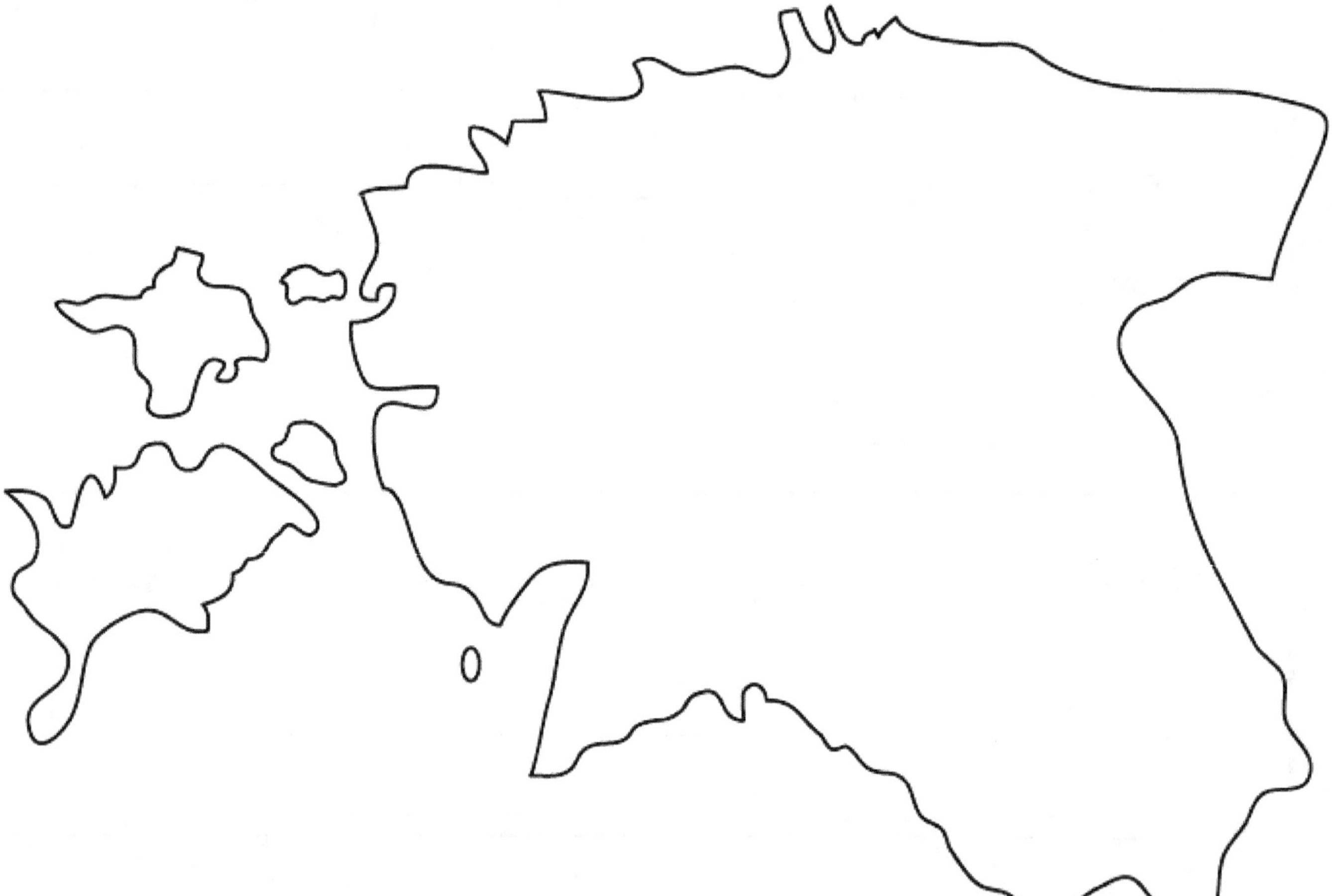

Label the capital city and any major physical features such as mountains, rivers, oceans or seas **in or around** this country.

Country Name: Estonia

Population:______________________________

Area: ___________________________________

Type of Government: __________________

Capital City: ____________________________

Religion(s): ______________________________

Language(s): _____________________________

Currency: ________________________________

Climate: _________________________________

Time Zone: ______________________________

Major Exports

1:_________________________

2: _________________________

3: _________________________

Mountains,
Rivers and Lakes

1:___________________________

2: __________________________

3: __________________________

Other Cool Things about this Country

1:____

2: ____

3: ____

4: ____

Finland

Color the country's flag in the box above.

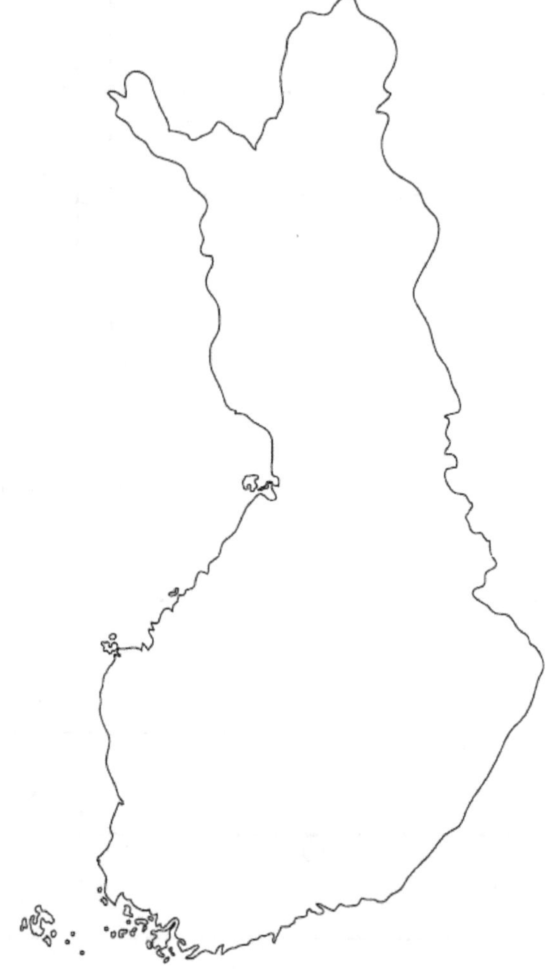

Label the capital city and any major physical features such as mountains, rivers, oceans or seas **in or around** this country.

Country Name: Finland

Population:__________________________

Area: ______________________________

Type of Government: ________________

Capital City: _________________________

Religion(s): __________________________

Language(s): _________________________

Currency: ___________________________

Climate: ____________________________

Time Zone: __________________________

Major Exports

1:_____________________

2: _____________________

3: _____________________

Mountains,
Rivers and Lakes

1:_______________________

2: ______________________

3: ______________________

Other Cool Things about this Country

1:____

2: ____

3: ____

4: ____

France

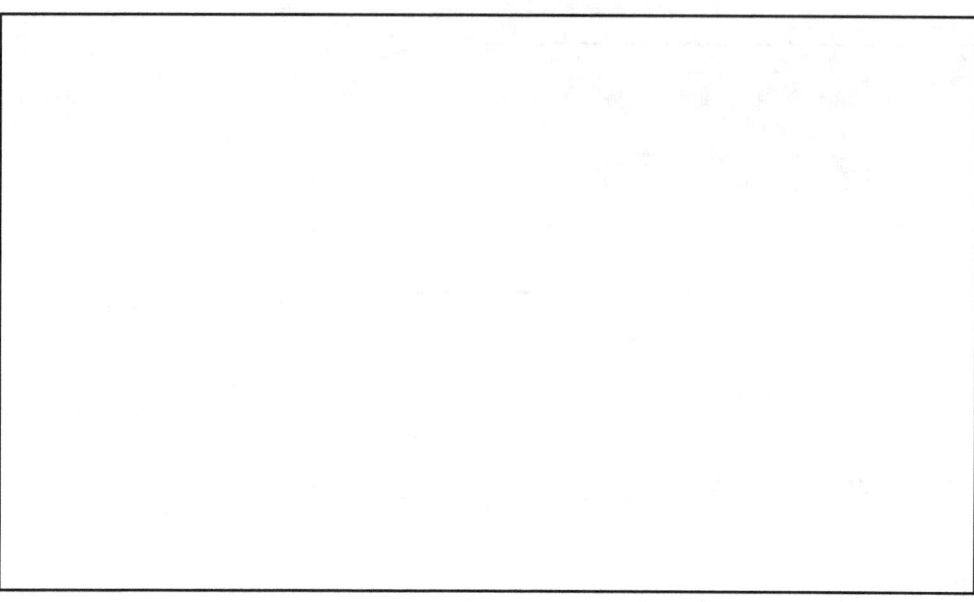

Color the country's flag in the box above.

Label the capital city and any major physical features such as mountains, rivers, oceans or seas **in or around** this country.

Country Name: France

Population:____________________

Area: ____________________

Type of Government: ____________

Capital City: ____________________

Religion(s): ____________________

Language(s): ____________________

Currency: ____________________

Climate: ____________________

Time Zone: ____________________

Major Exports

1:________________

2: ________________

3: ________________

Mountains, Rivers and Lakes

1:________________

2: ________________

3: ________________

Other Cool Things about this Country

1:____

2: ____

3: ____

4: ____

Germany

Color the country's flag in the box above.

Label the capital city and any major physical features such as mountains, rivers, oceans or seas **in or around** this country.

Country Name: Germany

Population: ____________________

Area: ____________________

Type of Government: ____________________

Capital City: ____________________

Religion(s): ____________________

Language(s): ____________________

Currency: ____________________

Climate: ____________________

Time Zone: ____________________

Major Exports

1: ____________________

2: ____________________

3: ____________________

Mountains, Rivers and Lakes

1: ____________________

2: ____________________

3: ____________________

Other Cool Things about this Country

1: ____________________

2: ____________________

3: ____________________

4: ____________________

Greece

Color the country's flag in the box above.

Label the capital city and any major physical features such as mountains, rivers, oceans or seas **in or around** this country.

Country Name: Greece

Population:__________________________

Area: ______________________________

Type of Government: ________________

Capital City: _________________________

Religion(s): __________________________

Language(s): _________________________

Currency: ___________________________

Climate: ____________________________

Time Zone: __________________________

Major Exports

1:______________________

2: ______________________

3: ______________________

Mountains, Rivers and Lakes

1:________________________

2: _______________________

3: _______________________

Other Cool Things about this Country

1:____

2: ____

3: ____

4: ____

Holy See (Vatican)

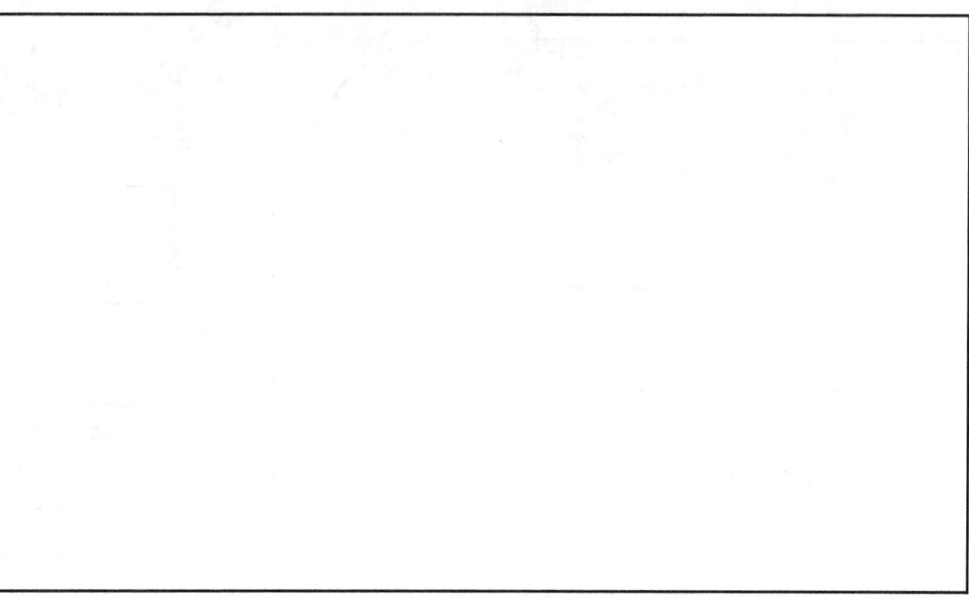

Color the country's flag in the box above.

Label the capital city and any major physical features such as mountains, rivers, oceans or seas **in or around** this country.

Country Name: Holy See

Population:____________________

Area: ____________________

Type of Government: ____________________

Capital City: ____________________

Religion(s): ____________________

Language(s): ____________________

Currency: ____________________

Climate: ____________________

Time Zone: ____________________

EXPORT

Major Exports

1:____________________

2: ____________________

3: ____________________

Mountains, Rivers and Lakes

1:____________________

2: ____________________

3: ____________________

Other Cool Things about this Country

1:____

2: ____

3: ____

4: ____

Hungary

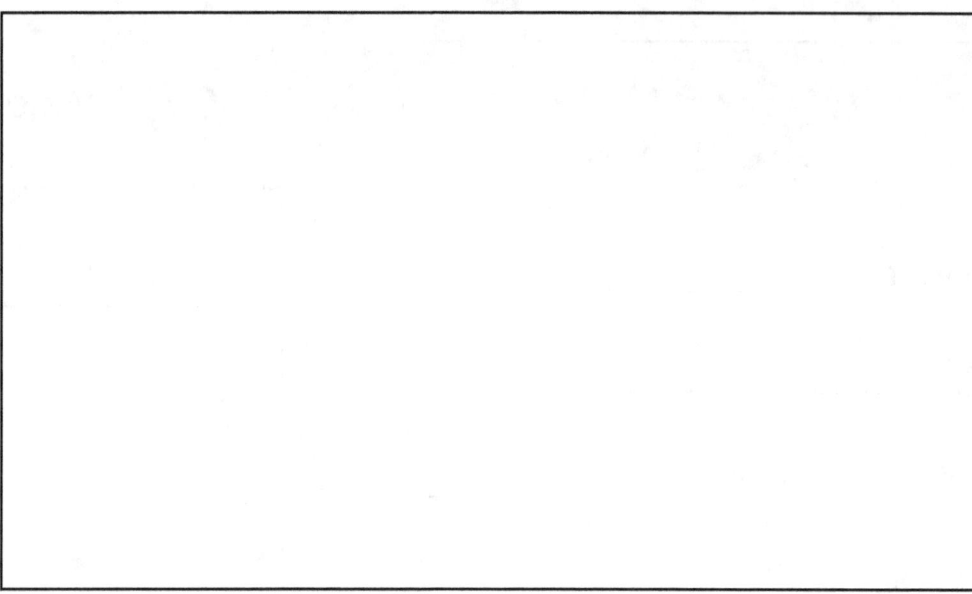

Color the country's flag in the box above.

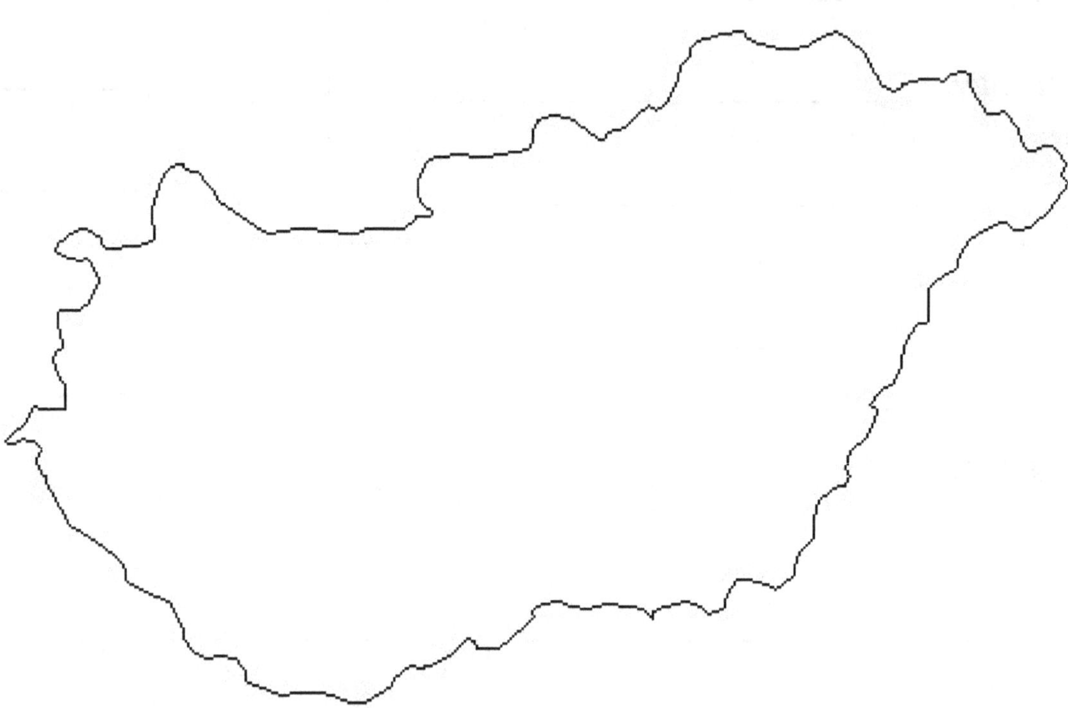

Label the capital city and any major physical features such as mountains, rivers, oceans or seas **in or around** this country.

Country Name: Hungary

Population:____________________________

Area: _________________________________

Type of Government: _________________

Capital City: ___________________________

Religion(s): _____________________________

Language(s): ___________________________

Currency: _____________________________

Climate: _______________________________

Time Zone: ____________________________

Major Exports

1:_______________________

2: _______________________

3: _______________________

Mountains, Rivers and Lakes

1:__________________________

2: _________________________

3: _________________________

Other Cool Things about this Country

1:____

2: ____

3: ____

4: ____

Iceland

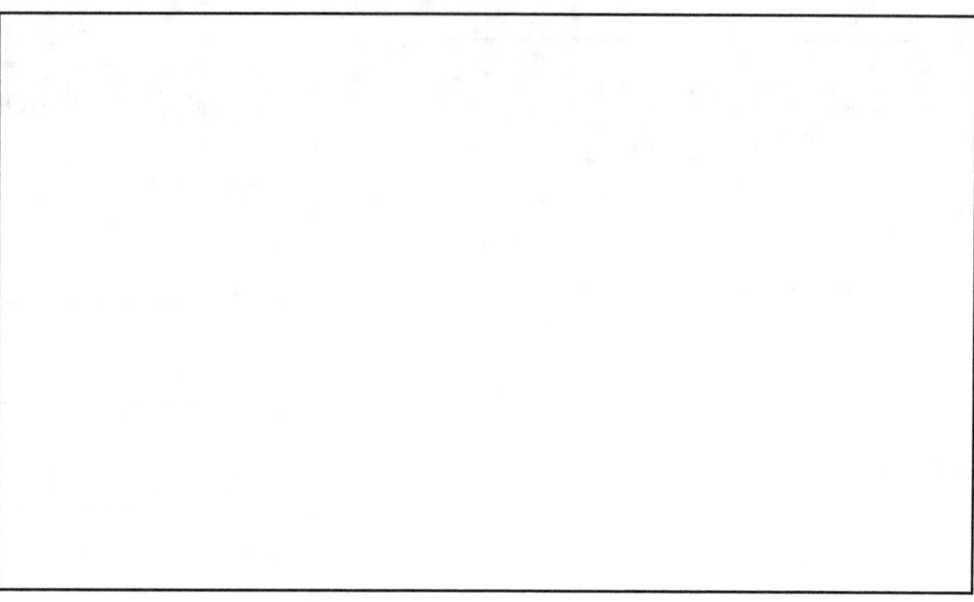

Color the country's flag in the box above.

Label the capital city and any major physical features such as mountains, rivers, oceans or seas **in or around** this country.

Country Name: Iceland

Population: ______________________

Area: ______________________

Type of Government: ______________

Capital City: ______________________

Religion(s): ______________________

Language(s): ______________________

Currency: ______________________

Climate: ______________________

Time Zone: ______________________

Major Exports

1: ______________________

2: ______________________

3: ______________________

Mountains, Rivers and Lakes

1: ______________________

2: ______________________

3: ______________________

Other Cool Things about this Country

1: ____

2: ____

3: ____

4: ____

Ireland

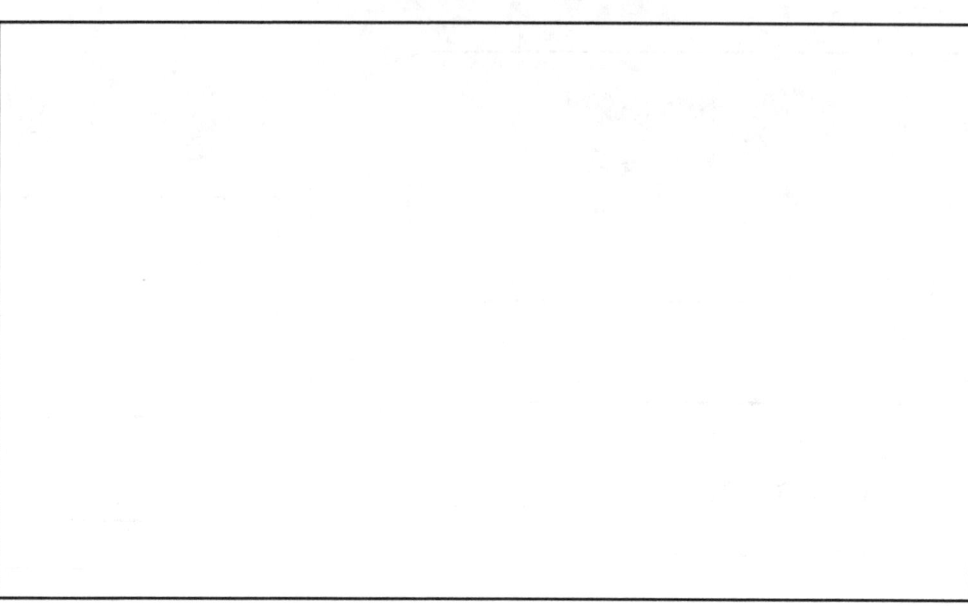

Color the country's flag in the box above.

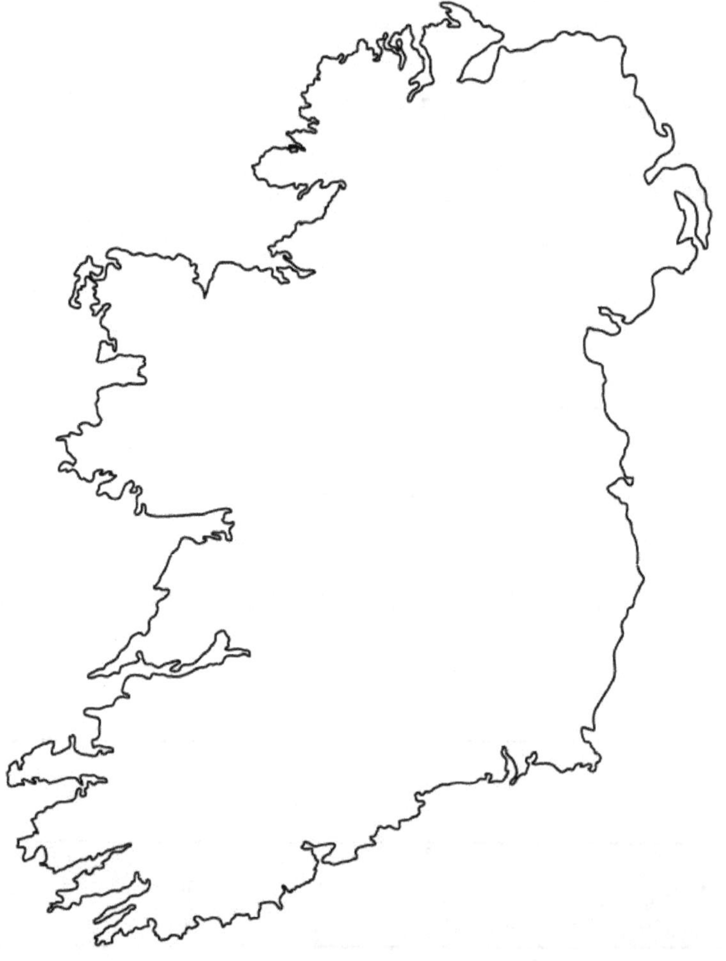

Label the capital city and any major physical features such as mountains, rivers, oceans or seas **in or around** this country.

Country Name: Ireland

Population: ______________________

Area: ______________________

Type of Government: ______________________

Capital City: ______________________

Religion(s): ______________________

Language(s): ______________________

Currency: ______________________

Climate: ______________________

Time Zone: ______________________

Major Exports

1: ______________________

2: ______________________

3: ______________________

Mountains, Rivers and Lakes

1: ______________________

2: ______________________

3: ______________________

Other Cool Things about this Country

1: ____

2: ____

3: ____

4: ____

Italy

Color the country's flag in the box above.

Label the capital city and any major physical features such as mountains, rivers, oceans or seas **in or around** this country.

Country Name: Italy

Population:________________________

Area: ___________________________

Type of Government: _______________

Capital City: _______________________

Religion(s): ________________________

Language(s): _______________________

Currency: _________________________

Climate: __________________________

Time Zone: ________________________

Major Exports

1:____________________

2: ____________________

3: ____________________

Mountains, Rivers and Lakes

1:______________________

2: _____________________

3: _____________________

Other Cool Things about this Country

1:____

2: ____

3: ____

4: ____

Latvia

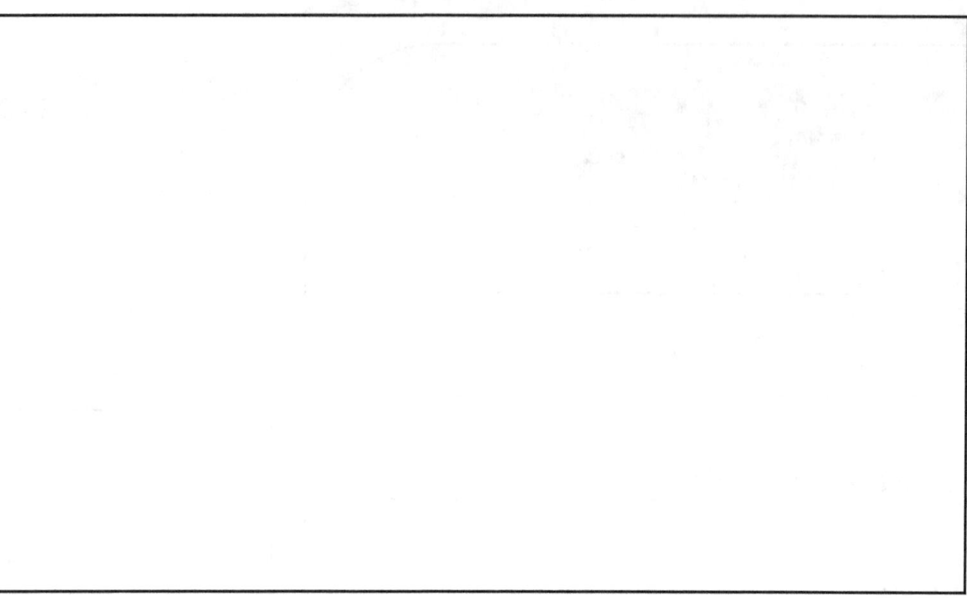

Color the country's flag in the box above.

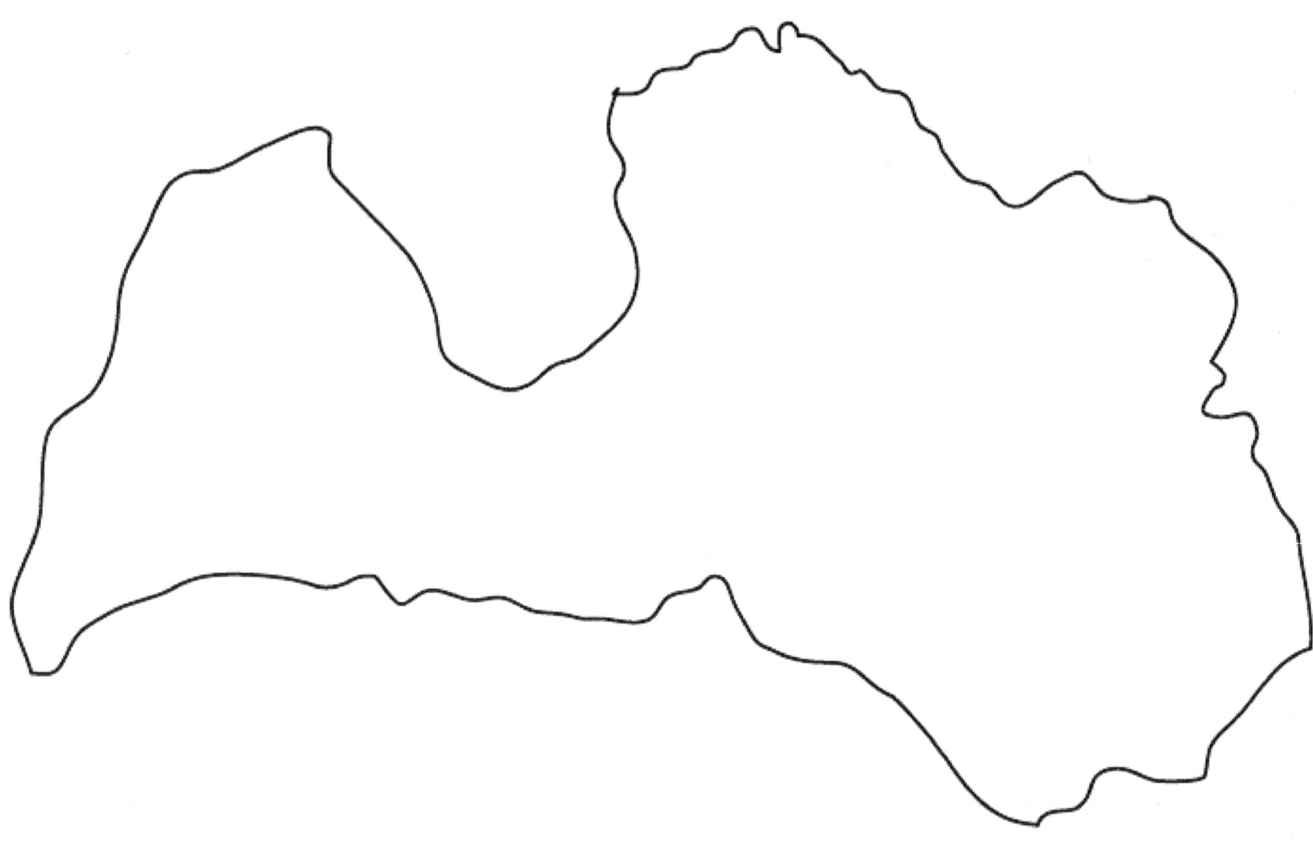

Label the capital city and any major physical features such as mountains, rivers, oceans or seas **in or around** this country.

Country Name: Latvia

Population: ____________________________

Area: ________________________________

Type of Government: _________________

Capital City: ___________________________

Religion(s): ___________________________

Language(s): ___________________________

Currency: ______________________________

Climate: _______________________________

Time Zone: ____________________________

Major Exports

1: _______________________

2: _______________________

3: _______________________

Mountains, Rivers and Lakes

1: _______________________

2: _______________________

3: _______________________

Other Cool Things about this Country

1: ____

2: ____

3: ____

4: ____

Liechtenstein

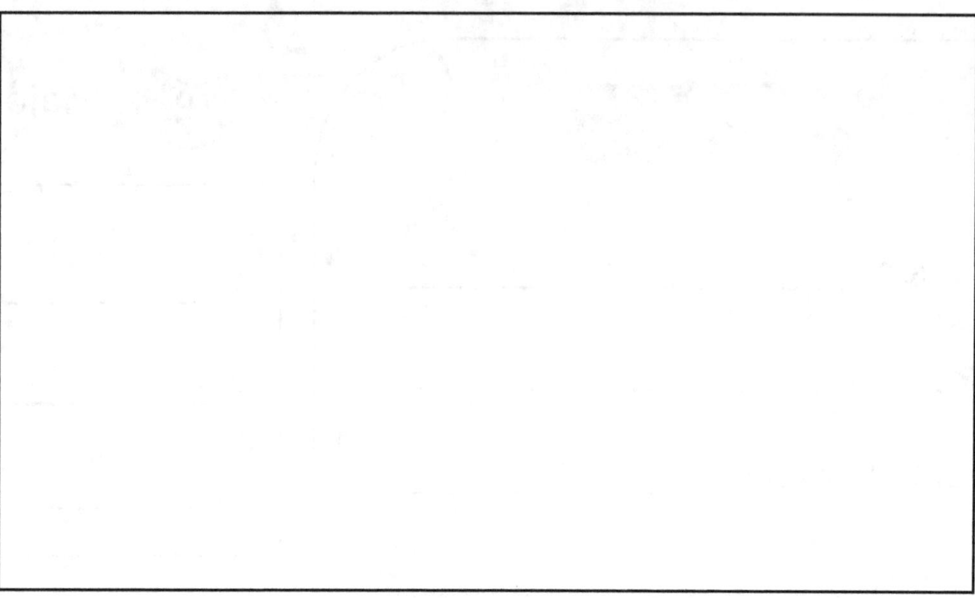

Color the country's flag in the box above.

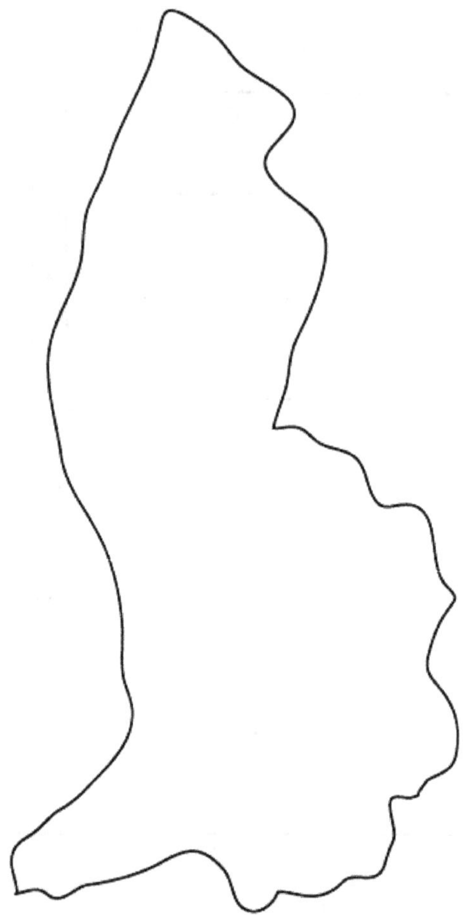

Label the capital city and any major physical features such as mountains, rivers, oceans or seas **in or around** this country.

Country Name: Liechtenstein

Population:________________________

Area: ____________________________

Type of Government: _______________

Capital City: _______________________

Religion(s): ________________________

Language(s): _______________________

Currency: _________________________

Climate: __________________________

Time Zone: ________________________

Major Exports

1:____________________

2: ____________________

3: ____________________

Mountains, Rivers and Lakes

1:______________________

2: _____________________

3: _____________________

Other Cool Things about this Country

1:____

2: ____

3: ____

4: ____

Lithuania

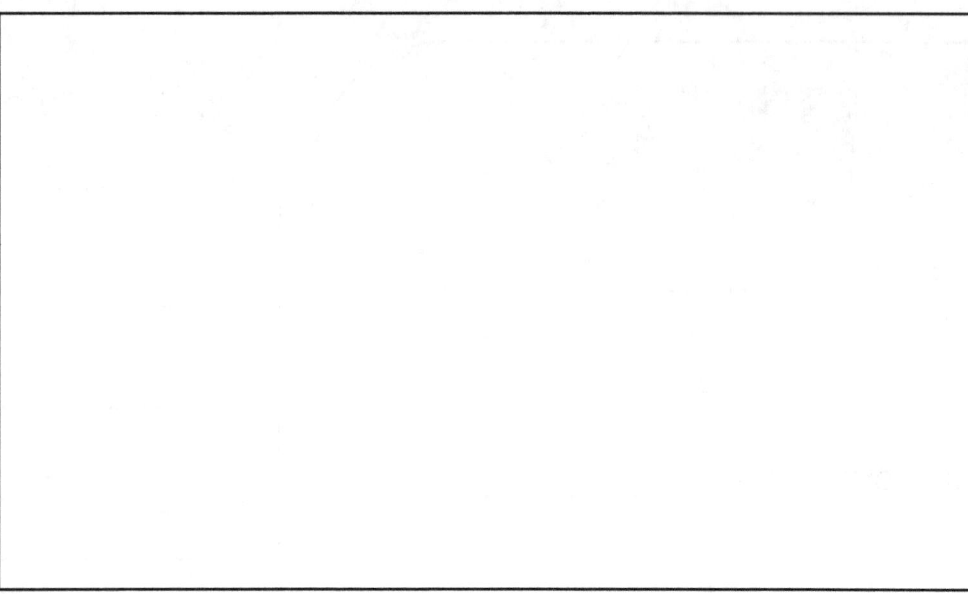

Color the country's flag in the box above.

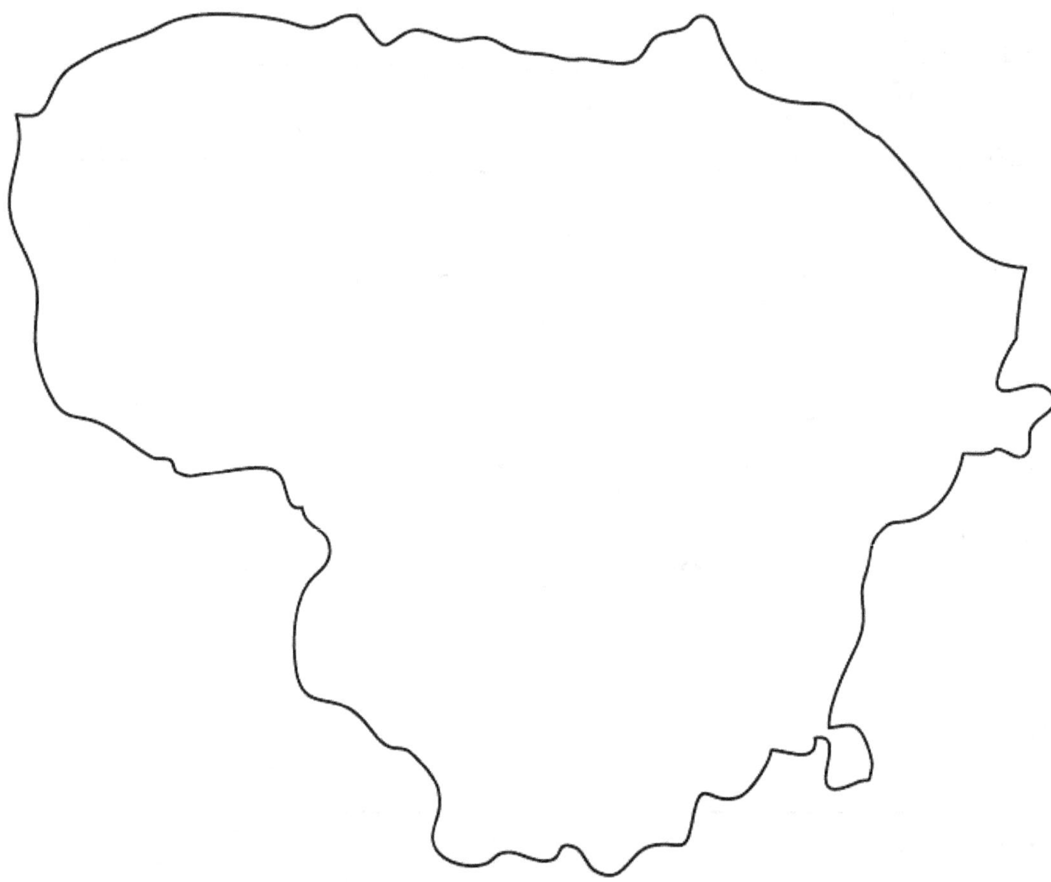

Label the capital city and any major physical features such as mountains, rivers, oceans or seas **in or around** this country.

Country Name: Lithuania

Population:________________________

Area: ___________________________

Type of Government: _______________

Capital City: _______________________

Religion(s): ________________________

Language(s): _______________________

Currency: _________________________

Climate: __________________________

Time Zone: ________________________

Major Exports

1:____________________

2: ____________________

3: ____________________

Mountains, Rivers and Lakes

1:______________________

2: _____________________

3: _____________________

Other Cool Things about this Country

1:____

2: ____

3: ____

4: ____

Luxembourg

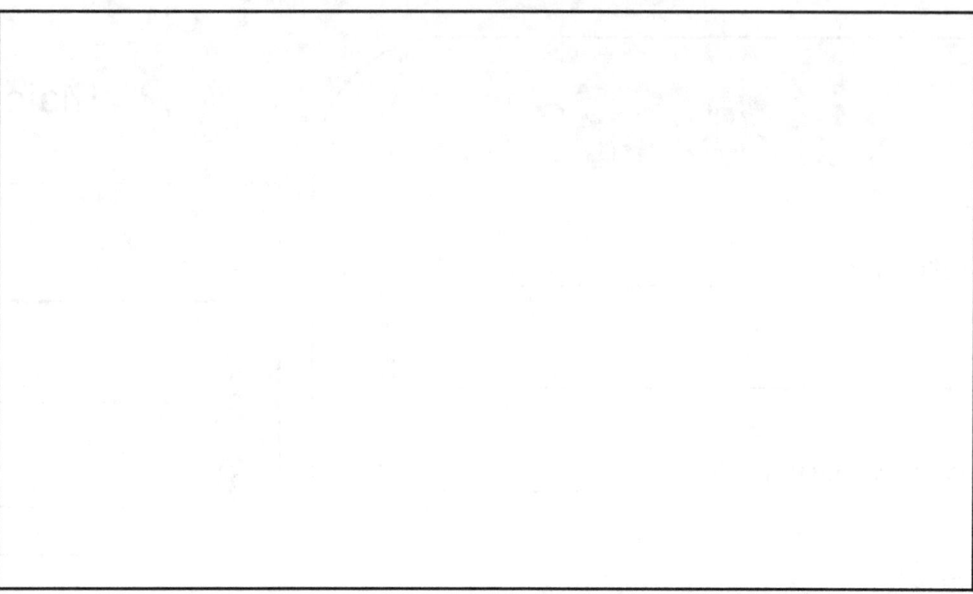

Color the country's flag in the box above.

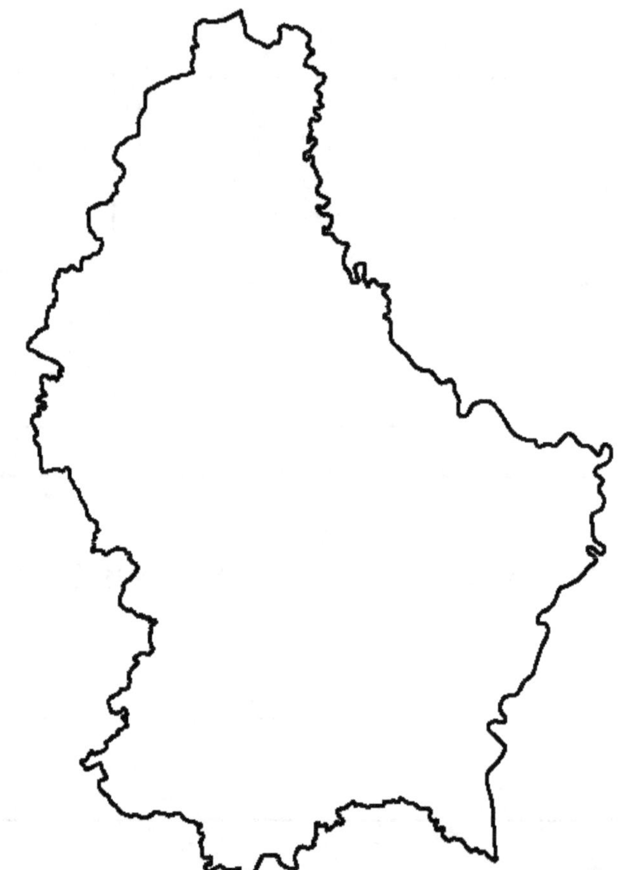

Label the capital city and any major physical features such as mountains, rivers, oceans or seas **in or around** this country.

Country Name: Luxembourg

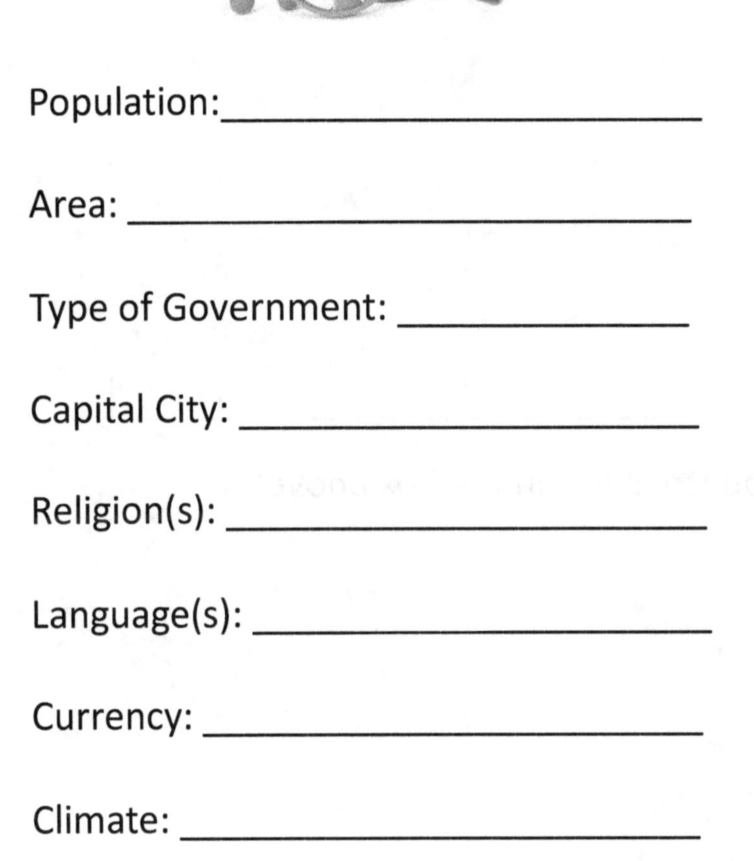

Population: ____________________

Area: ____________________

Type of Government: ____________________

Capital City: ____________________

Religion(s): ____________________

Language(s): ____________________

Currency: ____________________

Climate: ____________________

Time Zone: ____________________

Major Exports

1: ____________________

2: ____________________

3: ____________________

Mountains, Rivers and Lakes

1: ____________________

2: ____________________

3: ____________________

Other Cool Things about this Country

1: ____________________

2: ____________________

3: ____________________

4: ____________________

Malta

Color the country's flag in the box above.

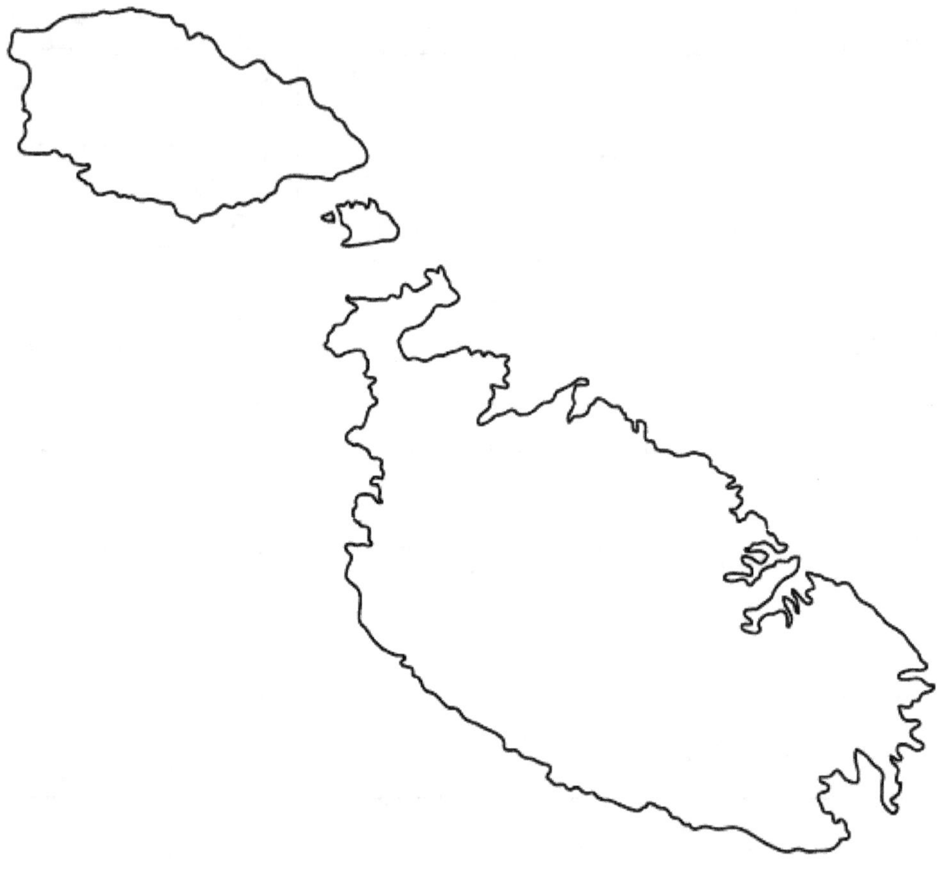

Label the capital city and any major physical features such as mountains, rivers, oceans or seas **in or around** this country.

Country Name: Malta

Population: ______________________

Area: ______________________

Type of Government: ______________

Capital City: ______________________

Religion(s): ______________________

Language(s): ______________________

Currency: ______________________

Climate: ______________________

Time Zone: ______________________

Major Exports

1: ______________________

2: ______________________

3: ______________________

Mountains, Rivers and Lakes

1: ______________________

2: ______________________

3: ______________________

Other Cool Things about this Country

1: ____

2: ____

3: ____

4: ____

Moldova

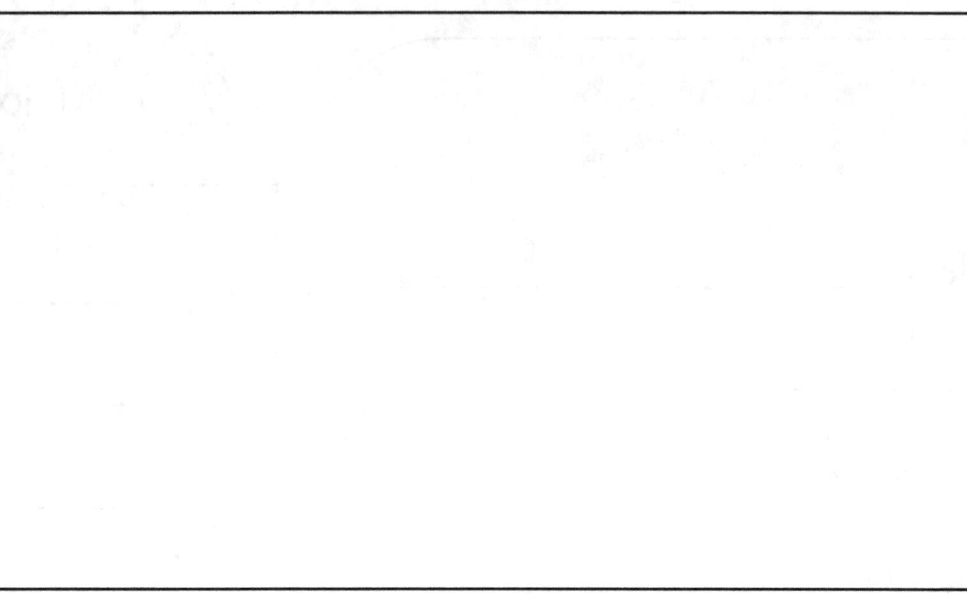

Color the country's flag in the box above.

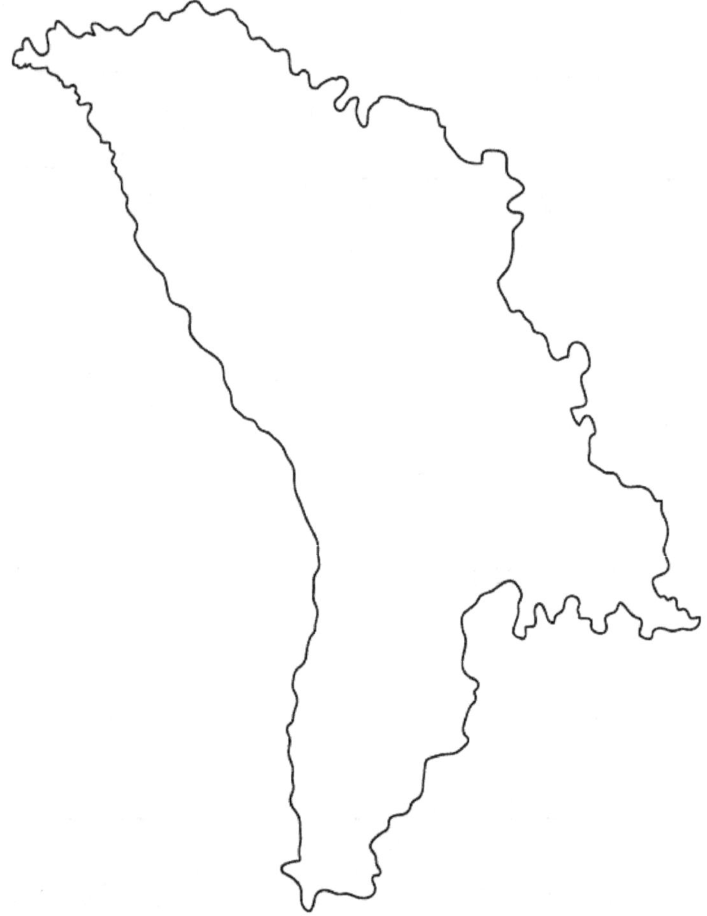

Label the capital city and any major physical features such as mountains, rivers, oceans or seas **in or around** this country.

Country Name: Moldova

Population:______________________

Area: ______________________

Type of Government: ______________

Capital City: ______________________

Religion(s): ______________________

Language(s): ______________________

Currency: ______________________

Climate: ______________________

Time Zone: ______________________

Major Exports

1:______________________

2: ______________________

3: ______________________

Mountains,
Rivers and Lakes

1:______________________

2: ______________________

3: ______________________

Other Cool Things about this Country

1:____

2: ____

3: ____

4: ____

Monaco

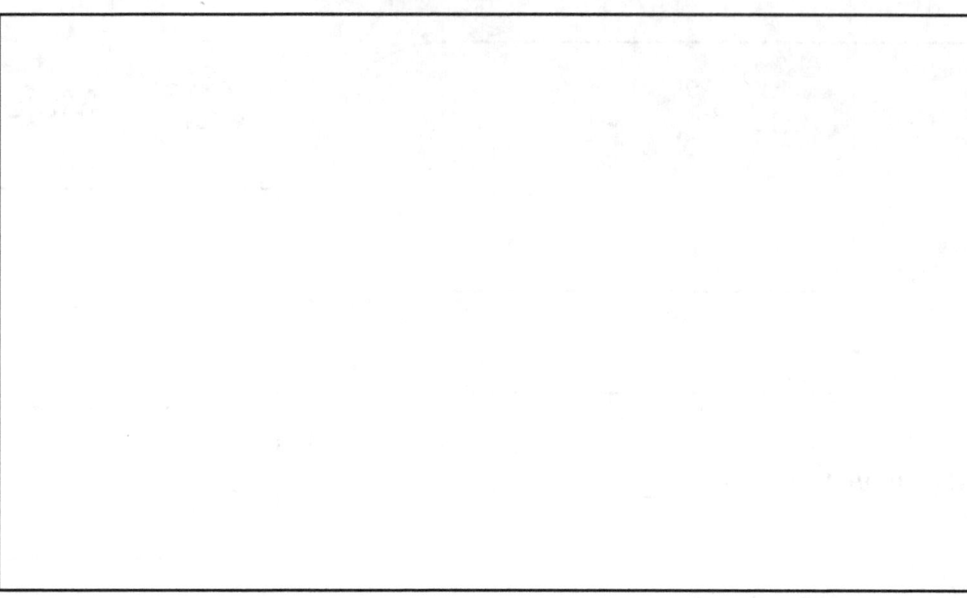

Color the country's flag in the box above.

Label the capital city and any major physical features such as mountains, rivers, oceans or seas **in or around** this country.

Country Name: Monaco

Population: ____________________

Area: ____________________

Type of Government: ____________________

Capital City: ____________________

Religion(s): ____________________

Language(s): ____________________

Currency: ____________________

Climate: ____________________

Time Zone: ____________________

Major Exports

1: ____________________

2: ____________________

3: ____________________

Mountains, Rivers and Lakes

1: ____________________

2: ____________________

3: ____________________

Other Cool Things about this Country

1: ____

2: ____

3: ____

4: ____

Montenegro

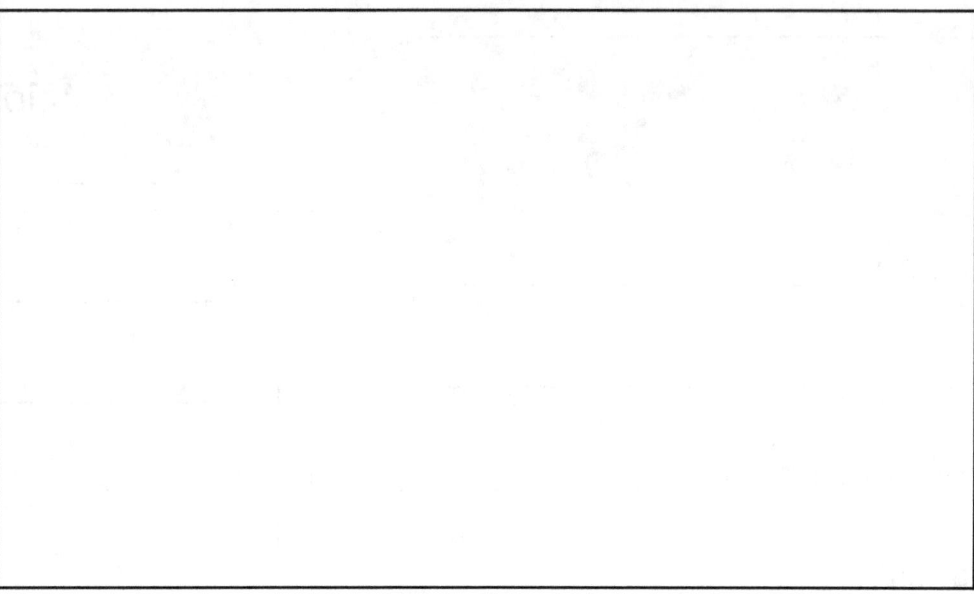

Color the country's flag in the box above.

Label the capital city and any major physical features such as mountains, rivers, oceans or seas **in or around** this country.

Country Name: Montenegro

Population:__________________________

Area: ______________________________

Type of Government: ________________

Capital City: _________________________

Religion(s): __________________________

Language(s): _________________________

Currency: ___________________________

Climate: _____________________________

Time Zone: ___________________________

Major Exports

1:______________________

2: ______________________

3: ______________________

Mountains, Rivers and Lakes

1:________________________

2: _______________________

3: _______________________

Other Cool Things about this Country

1:____

2: ____

3: ____

4: ____

Netherlands

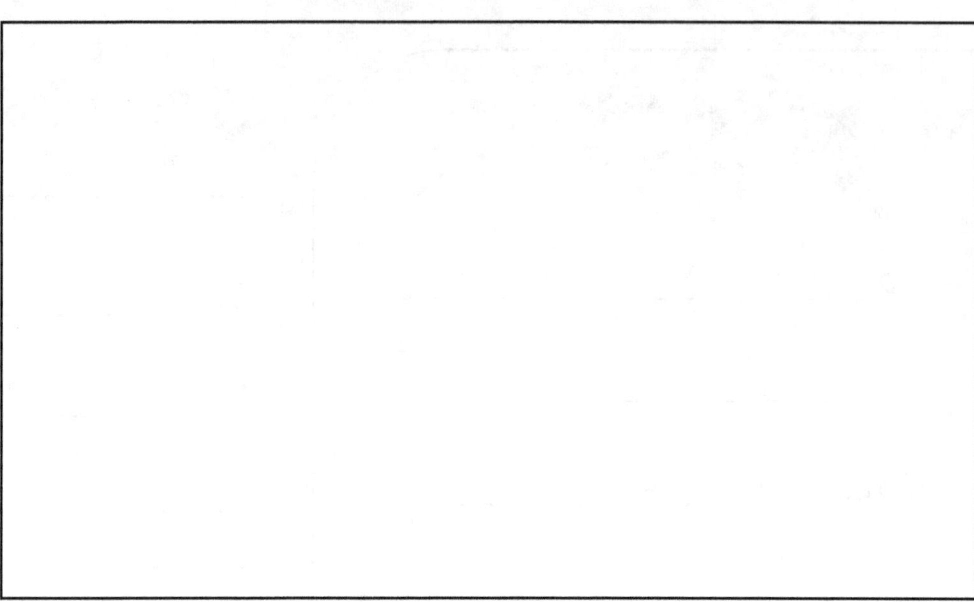

Color the country's flag in the box above.

Label the capital city and any major physical features such as mountains, rivers, oceans or seas **in or around** this country.

Country Name: Netherlands

Population:________________________

Area: ____________________________

Type of Government: _______________

Capital City: _______________________

Religion(s): ________________________

Language(s): _______________________

Currency: _________________________

Climate: __________________________

Time Zone: ________________________

Major Exports

1:____________________

2: ____________________

3: ____________________

Mountains, Rivers and Lakes

1:____________________

2: ____________________

3: ____________________

Other Cool Things about this Country

1:____

2: ____

3: ____

4: ____

North Macedonia

Color the country's flag in the box above.

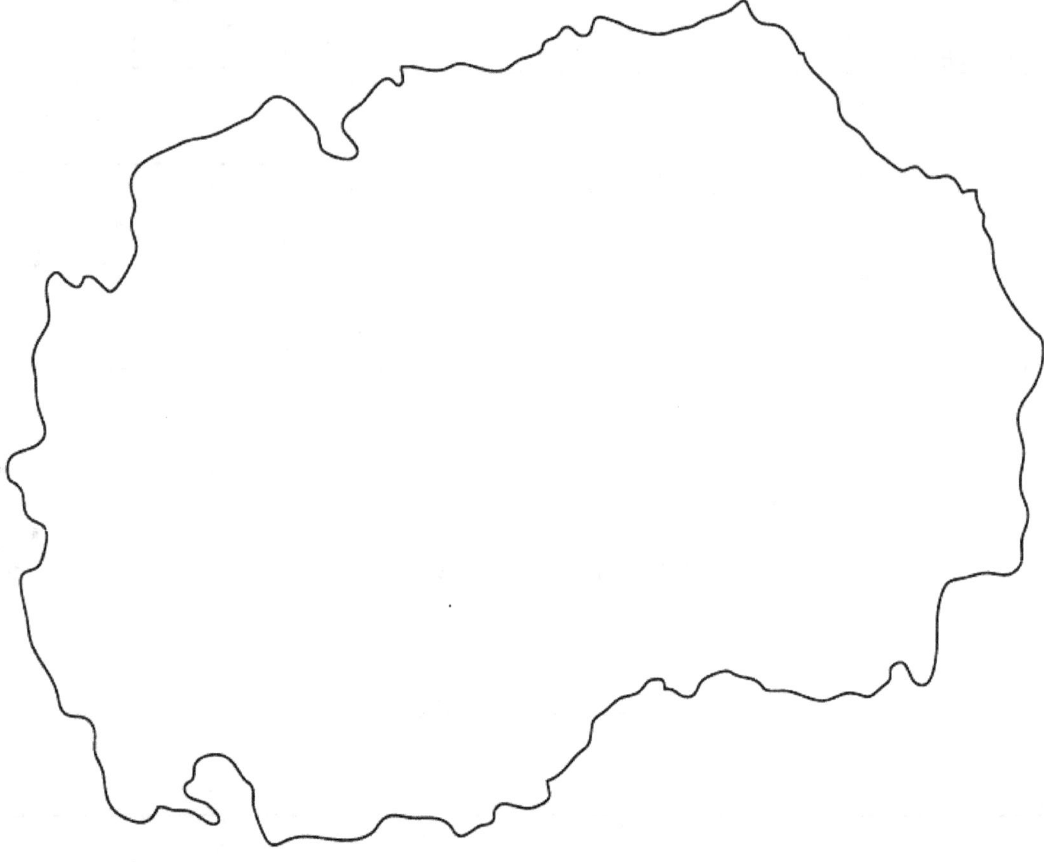

Label the capital city and any major physical features such as mountains, rivers, oceans or seas **in or around** this country.

Country Name: North Macedonia

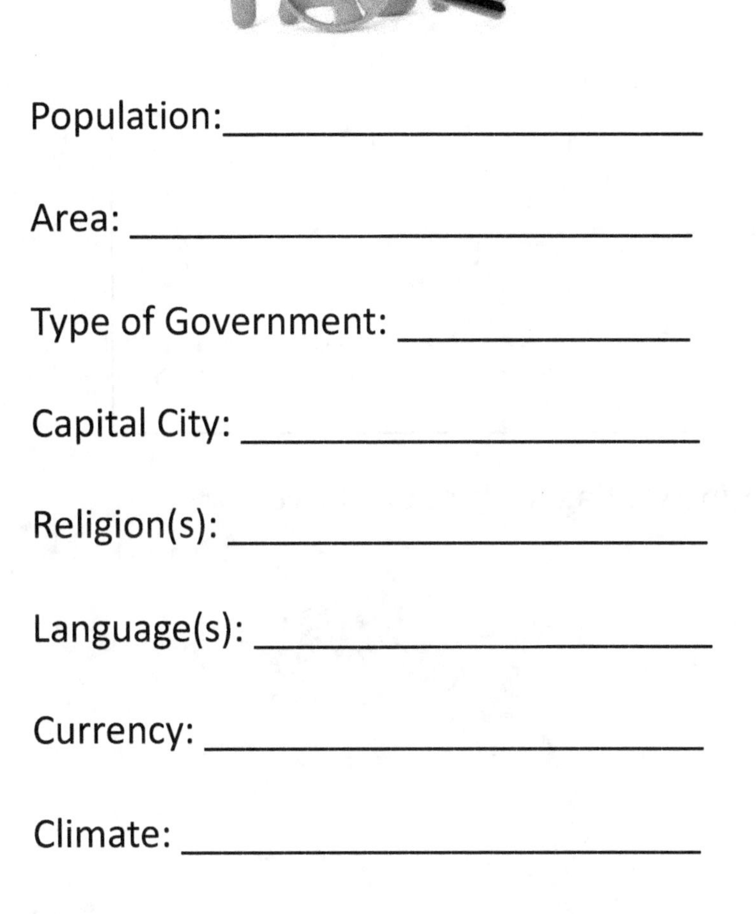

Population: ______________________

Area: ______________________

Type of Government: ______________

Capital City: ____________________

Religion(s): _____________________

Language(s): ____________________

Currency: _______________________

Climate: ________________________

Time Zone: ______________________

Major Exports

1: ____________________

2: ____________________

3: ____________________

Mountains, Rivers and Lakes

1: ____________________

2: ____________________

3: ____________________

Other Cool Things about this Country

1: ____

2: ____

3: ____

4: ____

Norway

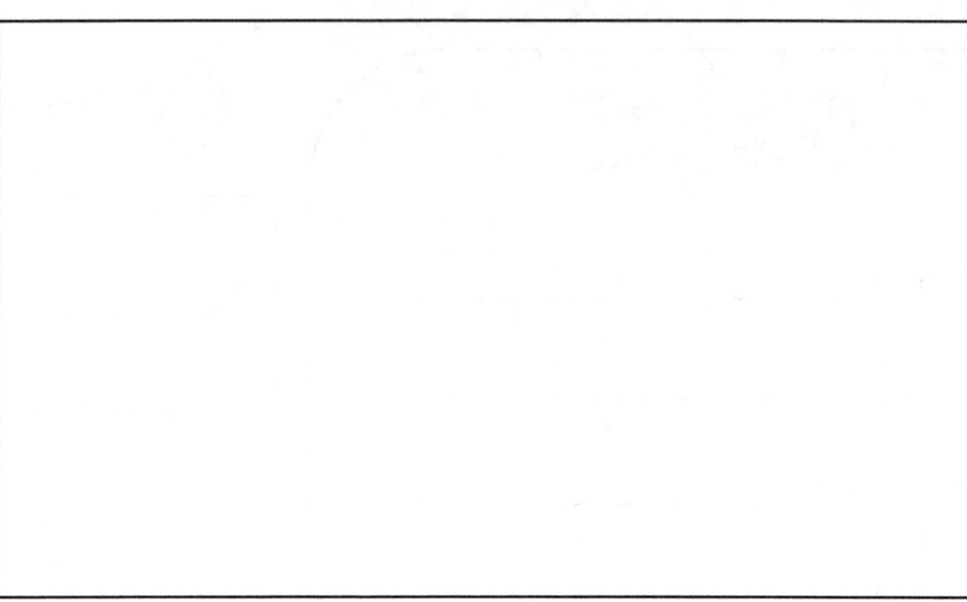

Color the country's flag in the box above.

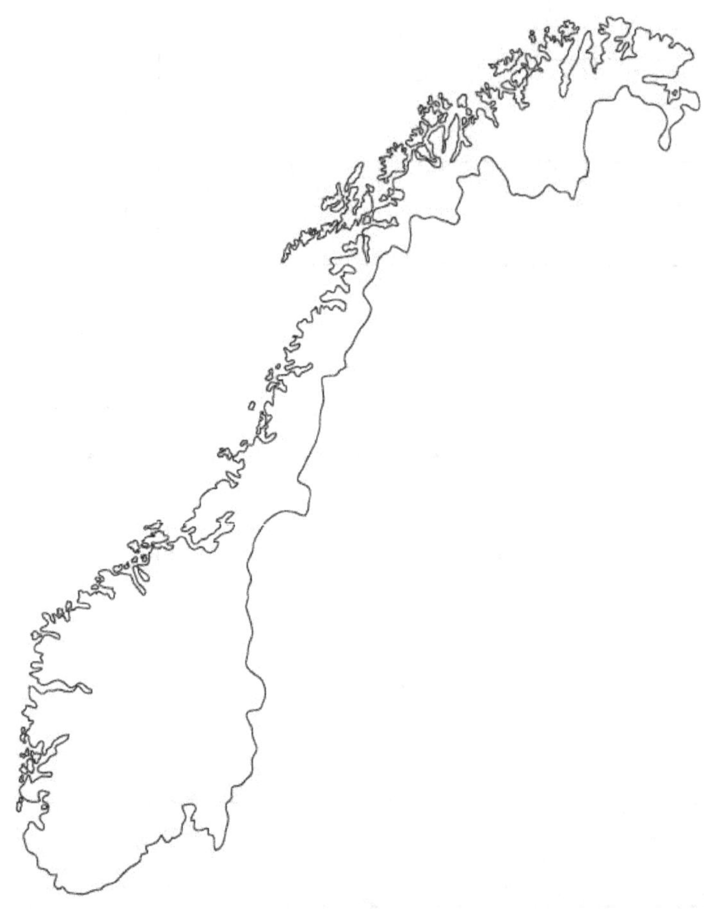

Label the capital city and any major physical features such as mountains, rivers, oceans or seas **in or around** this country.

Country Name: Norway

Population:____________________

Area: ____________________

Type of Government: ____________________

Capital City: ____________________

Religion(s): ____________________

Language(s): ____________________

Currency: ____________________

Climate: ____________________

Time Zone: ____________________

Major Exports

1:____________________

2: ____________________

3: ____________________

Mountains, Rivers and Lakes

1:____________________

2: ____________________

3: ____________________

Other Cool Things about this Country

1:____

2: ____

3: ____

4: ____

Poland

Color the country's flag in the box above.

Label the capital city and any major physical features such as mountains, rivers, oceans or seas **in or around** this country.

Country Name: Poland

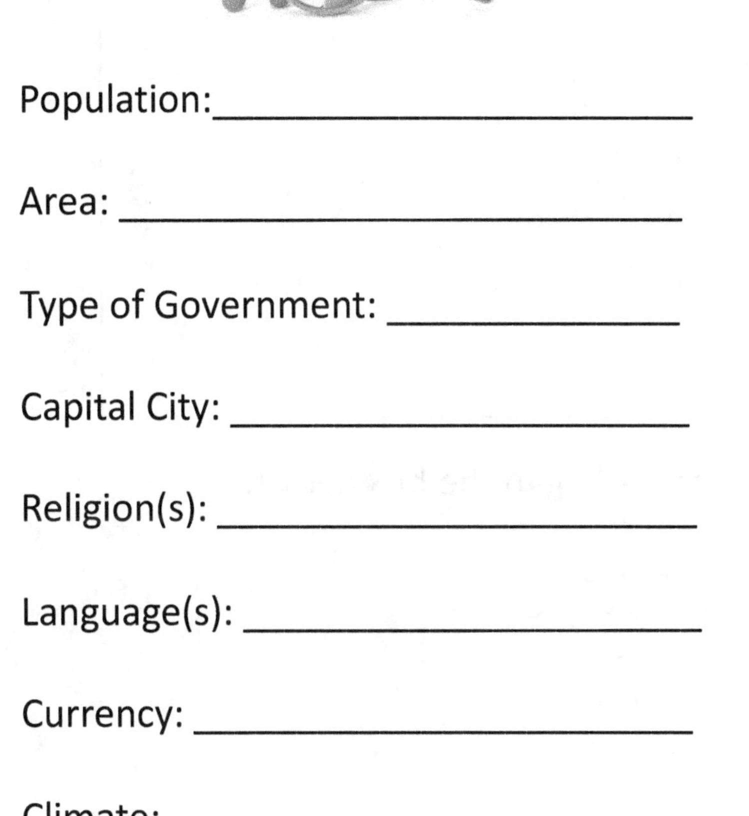

Population:______________________

Area: ______________________

Type of Government: ______________

Capital City: ______________________

Religion(s): ______________________

Language(s): ______________________

Currency: ______________________

Climate: ______________________

Time Zone: ______________________

Major Exports

1:__________________

2: __________________

3: __________________

Mountains,
Rivers and Lakes

1:__________________

2: __________________

3: __________________

Other Cool Things about this Country

1:____

2: ____

3: ____

4: ____

Portugal

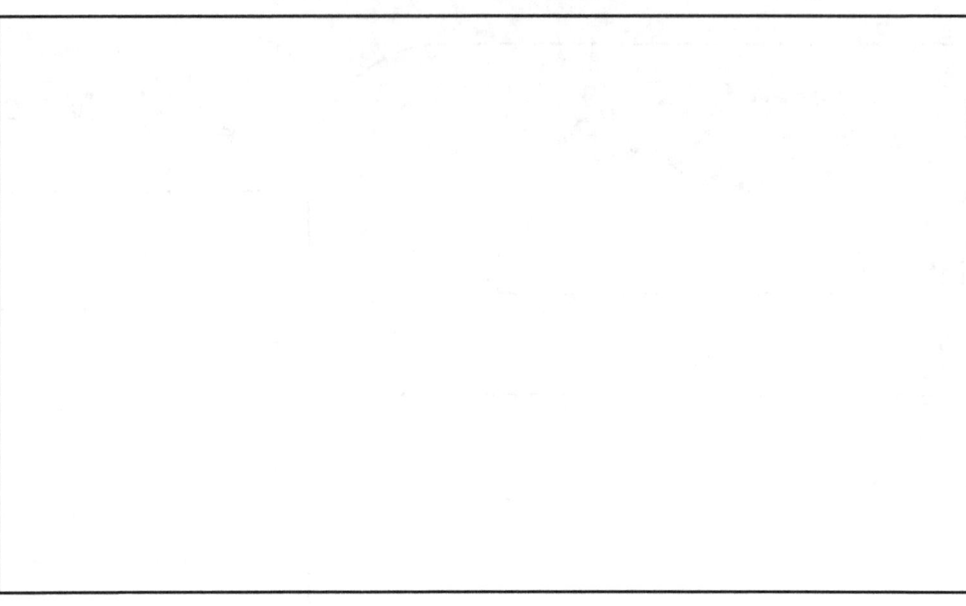

Color the country's flag in the box above.

Label the capital city and any major physical features such as mountains, rivers, oceans or seas **in or around** this country.

Country Name: Portugal

Population:_________________________

Area: ______________________________

Type of Government: _______________

Capital City: ________________________

Religion(s): _________________________

Language(s): ________________________

Currency: ___________________________

Climate: ____________________________

Time Zone: __________________________

Major Exports

1: _____________________

2: _____________________

3: _____________________

Mountains, Rivers and Lakes

1: _______________________

2: ______________________

3: ______________________

Other Cool Things about this Country

1: ____

2: ____

3: ____

4: ____

Romania

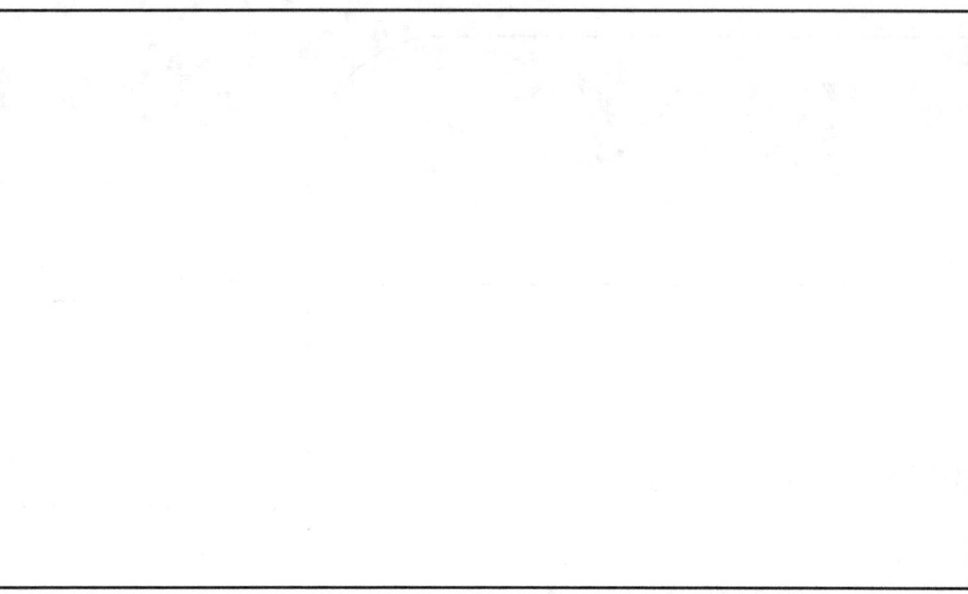

Color the country's flag in the box above.

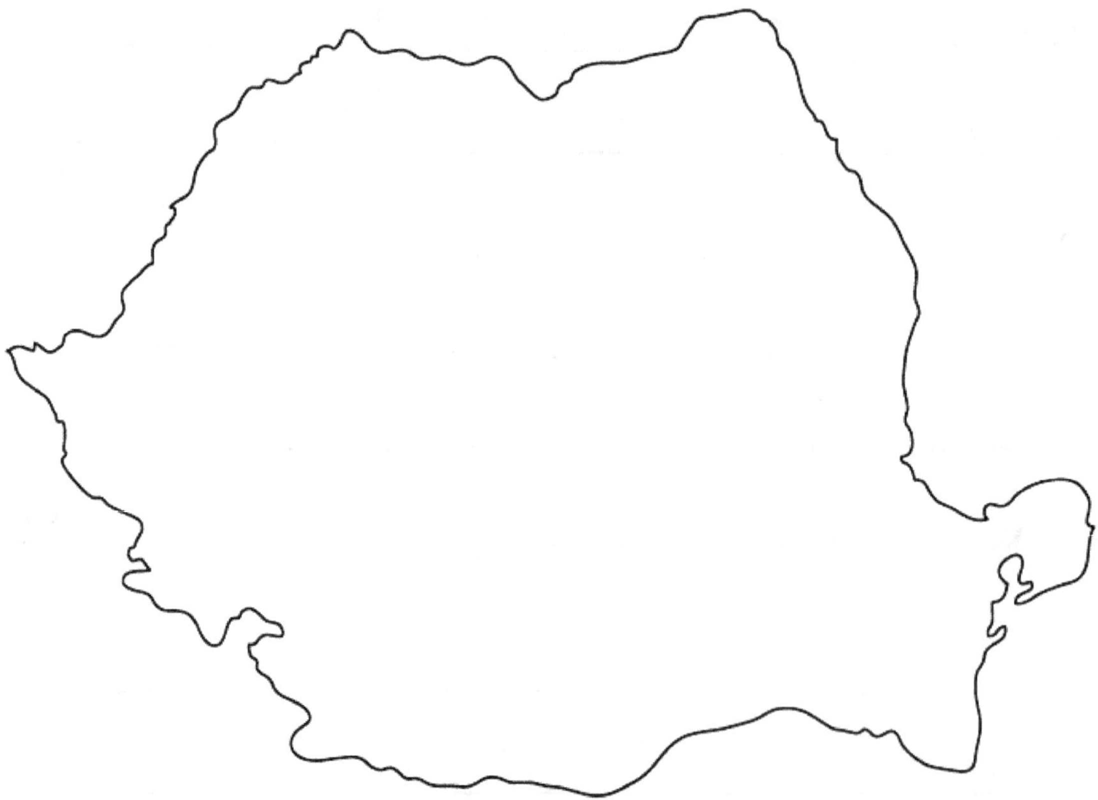

Label the capital city and any major physical features such as mountains, rivers, oceans or seas **in or around** this country.

Country Name: Romania

Population:________________________

Area: ________________________

Type of Government: ________________

Capital City: ________________________

Religion(s): ________________________

Language(s): ________________________

Currency: ________________________

Climate: ________________________

Time Zone: ________________________

Major Exports

1:____________________

2: ____________________

3: ____________________

Mountains, Rivers and Lakes

1:____________________

2: ____________________

3: ____________________

Other Cool Things about this Country

1:____

2: ____

3: ____

4: ____

Russia

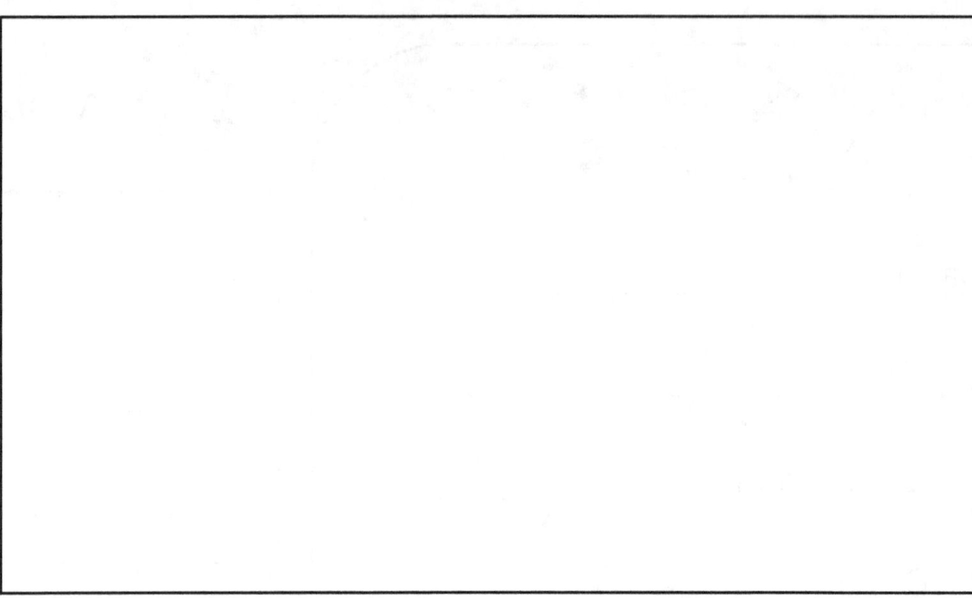

Color the country's flag in the box above.

Label the capital city and any major physical features such as mountains, rivers, oceans or seas **in or around** this country.

Country Name: Russia

Population:__________________________

Area: ______________________________

Type of Government: ________________

Capital City: _________________________

Religion(s): __________________________

Language(s): _________________________

Currency: ___________________________

Climate: ____________________________

Time Zone: __________________________

Major Exports

1:_____________________

2: _____________________

3: _____________________

Mountains, Rivers and Lakes

1:_______________________

2: ______________________

3: ______________________

Other Cool Things about this Country

1:____

2: ____

3: ____

4: ____

San Marino

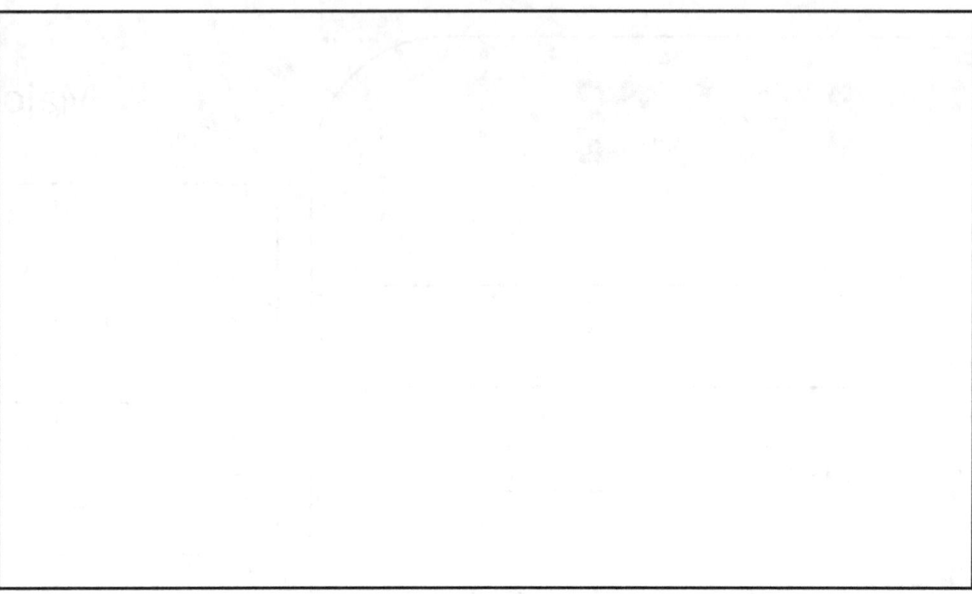

Color the country's flag in the box above.

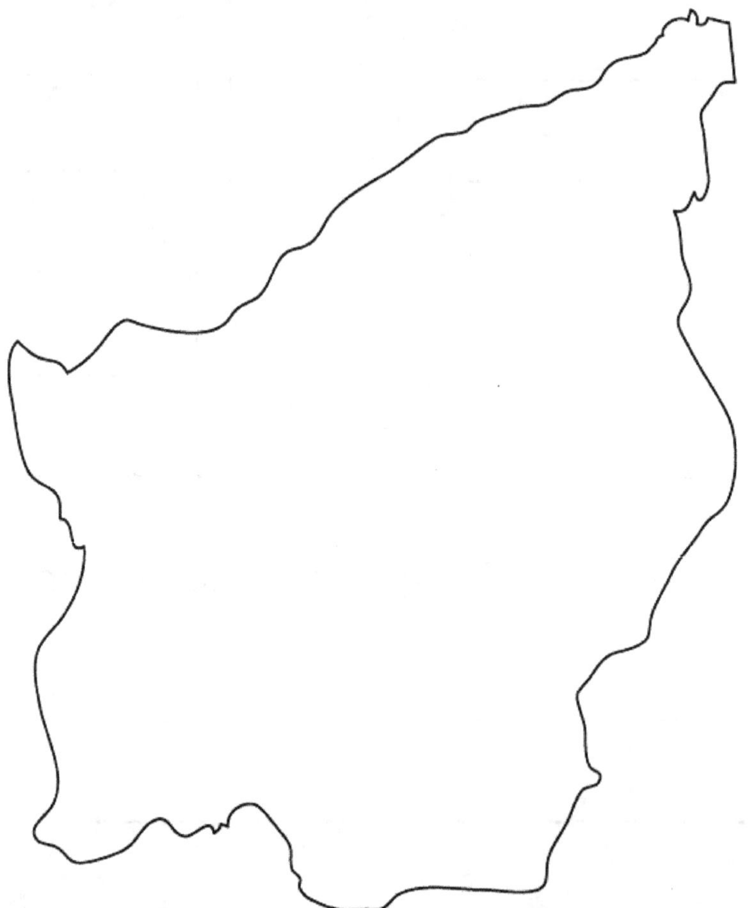

Label the capital city and any major physical features such as mountains, rivers, oceans or seas **in or around** this country.

Country Name: San Marino

Population: ______________________

Area: ______________________

Type of Government: ______________

Capital City: ______________________

Religion(s): ______________________

Language(s): ______________________

Currency: ______________________

Climate: ______________________

Time Zone: ______________________

Major Exports

1: ______________________

2: ______________________

3: ______________________

Mountains, Rivers and Lakes

1: ______________________

2: ______________________

3: ______________________

Other Cool Things about this Country

1: ____

2: ____

3: ____

4: ____

Serbia

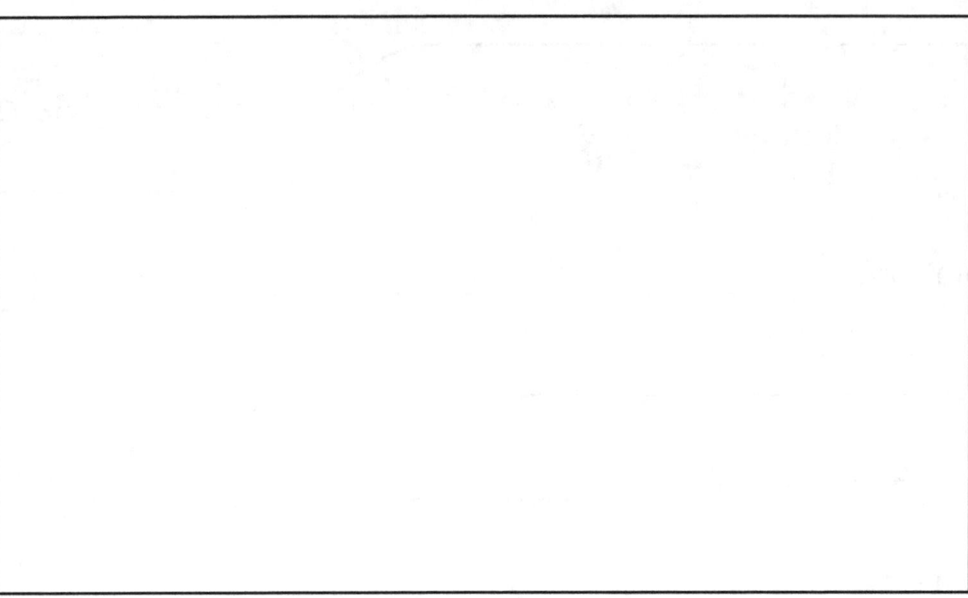

Color the country's flag in the box above.

Label the capital city and any major physical features such as mountains, rivers, oceans or seas **in or around** this country.

Country Name: Serbia

Population:______________________

Area: ______________________

Type of Government: ______________

Capital City: ______________________

Religion(s): ______________________

Language(s): ______________________

Currency: ______________________

Climate: ______________________

Time Zone: ______________________

Major Exports

1:______________________

2: ______________________

3: ______________________

Mountains, Rivers and Lakes

1:______________________

2: ______________________

3: ______________________

Other Cool Things about this Country

1:____

2: ____

3: ____

4: ____

Slovakia

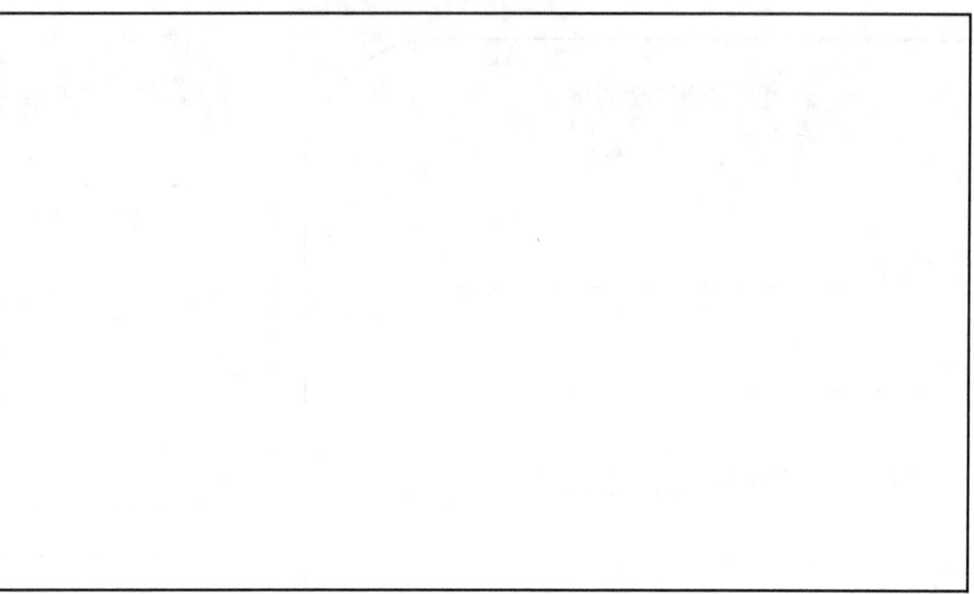

Color the country's flag in the box above.

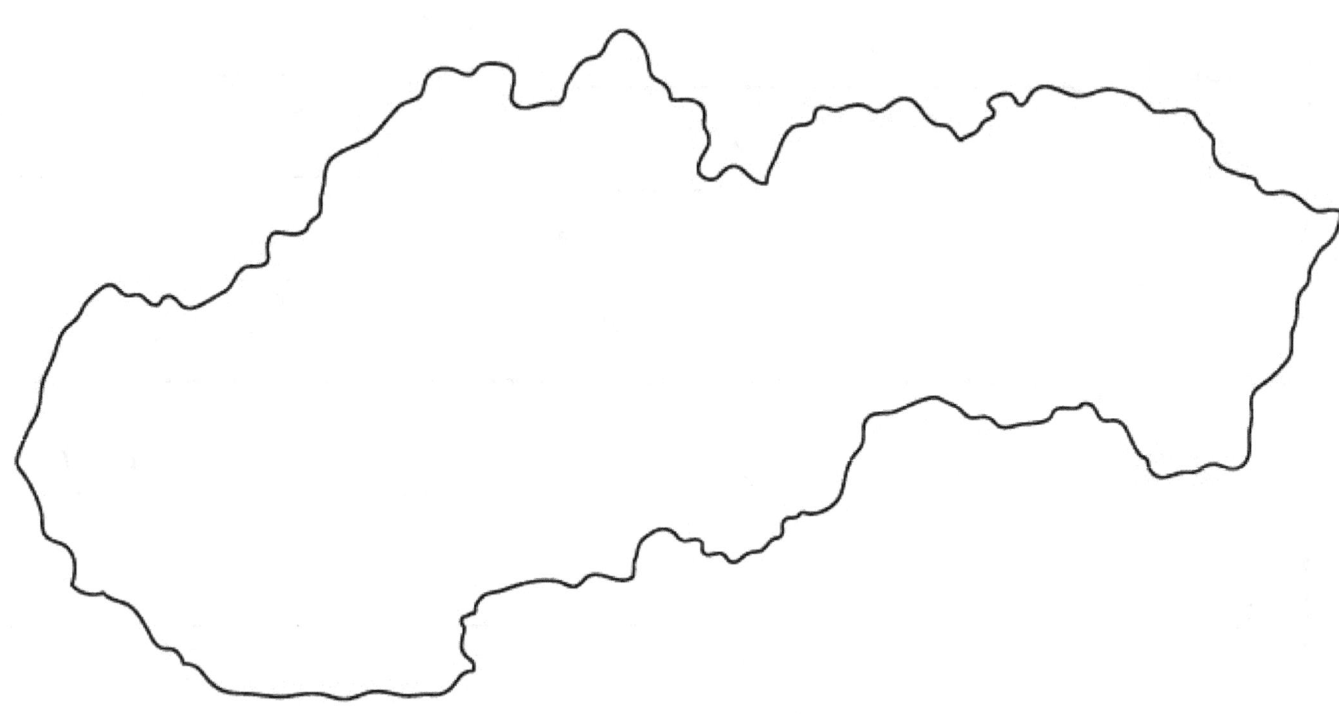

Label the capital city and any major physical features such as mountains, rivers, oceans or seas **in or around** this country.

Country Name: Slovakia

Population:____________________________

Area: ________________________________

Type of Government: _________________

Capital City: ___________________________

Religion(s): _____________________________

Language(s): ___________________________

Currency: _____________________________

Climate: ______________________________

Time Zone: ____________________________

Major Exports

1:_______________________

2: _______________________

3: _______________________

Mountains, Rivers and Lakes

1:_________________________

2: ________________________

3: ________________________

Other Cool Things about this Country

1:____

2: ____

3: ____

4: ____

Slovenia

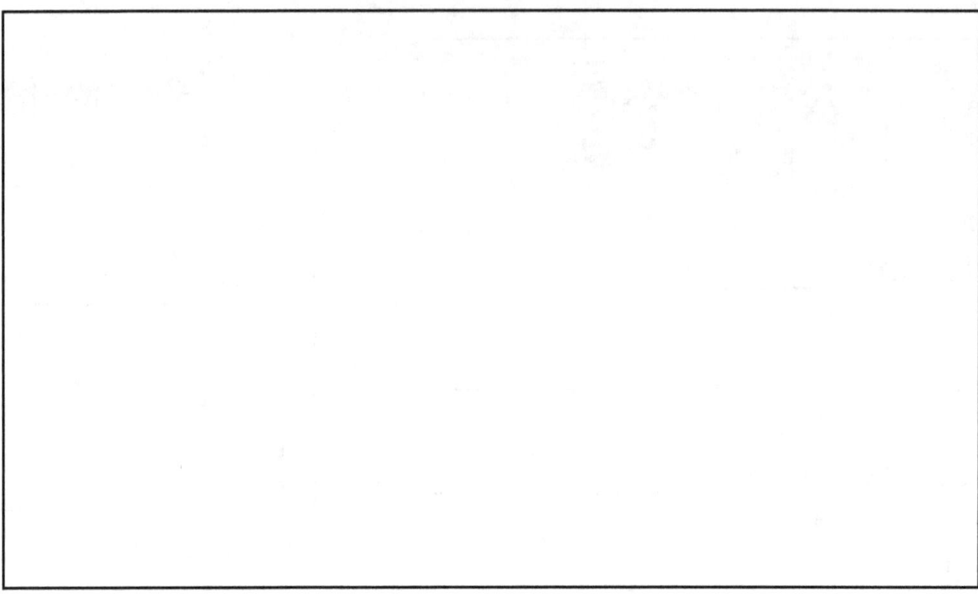

Color the country's flag in the box above.

Label the capital city and any major physical features such as mountains, rivers, oceans or seas **in or around** this country.

Country Name: Slovenia

Population:____________________

Area: ____________________

Type of Government: ____________

Capital City: ____________________

Religion(s): ____________________

Language(s): ____________________

Currency: ____________________

Climate: ____________________

Time Zone: ____________________

Major Exports

1:____________________

2: ____________________

3: ____________________

Mountains, Rivers and Lakes

1:____________________

2: ____________________

3: ____________________

Other Cool Things about this Country

1:____

2: ____

3: ____

4: ____

Spain

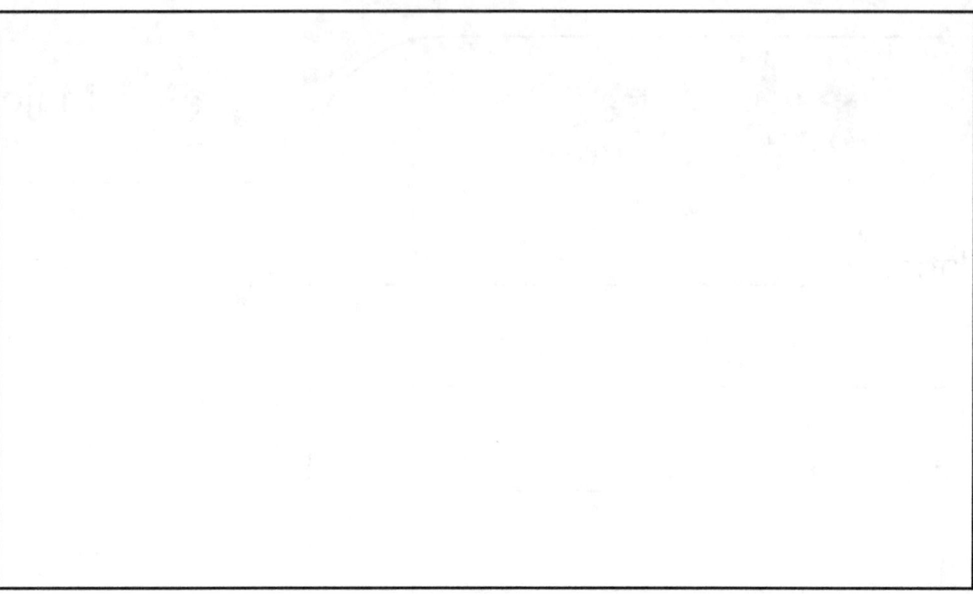

Color the country's flag in the box above.

Label the capital city and any major physical features such as mountains, rivers, oceans or seas **in or around** this country.

Country Name: Spain

Population:____________________

Area: ____________________

Type of Government: ____________________

Capital City: ____________________

Religion(s): ____________________

Language(s): ____________________

Currency: ____________________

Climate: ____________________

Time Zone: ____________________

Major Exports

1: ____________________

2: ____________________

3: ____________________

Mountains, Rivers and Lakes

1: ____________________

2: ____________________

3: ____________________

Other Cool Things about this Country

1: ____

2: ____

3: ____

4: ____

Sweden

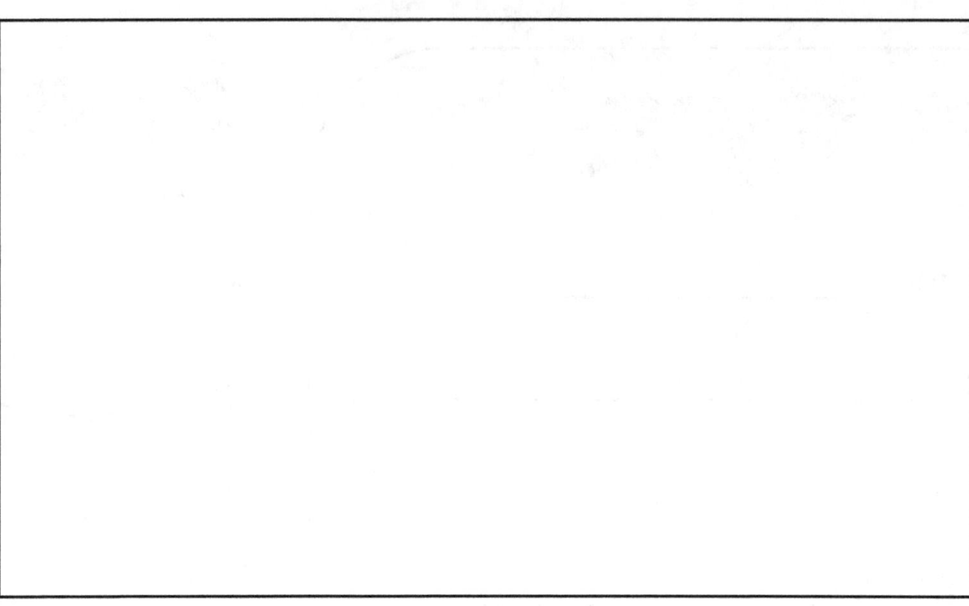

Color the country's flag in the box above.

Label the capital city and any major physical features such as mountains, rivers, oceans or seas **in or around** this country.

Country Name: Sweden

Population:________________________

Area: ____________________________

Type of Government: _______________

Capital City: _______________________

Religion(s): ________________________

Language(s): _______________________

Currency: _________________________

Climate: __________________________

Time Zone: ________________________

Major Exports

1:____________________

2: ____________________

3: ____________________

Mountains,
Rivers and Lakes

1:______________________

2: _____________________

3: _____________________

Other Cool Things about this Country

1:____

2: ____

3: ____

4: ____

Switzerland

Color the country's flag in the box above.

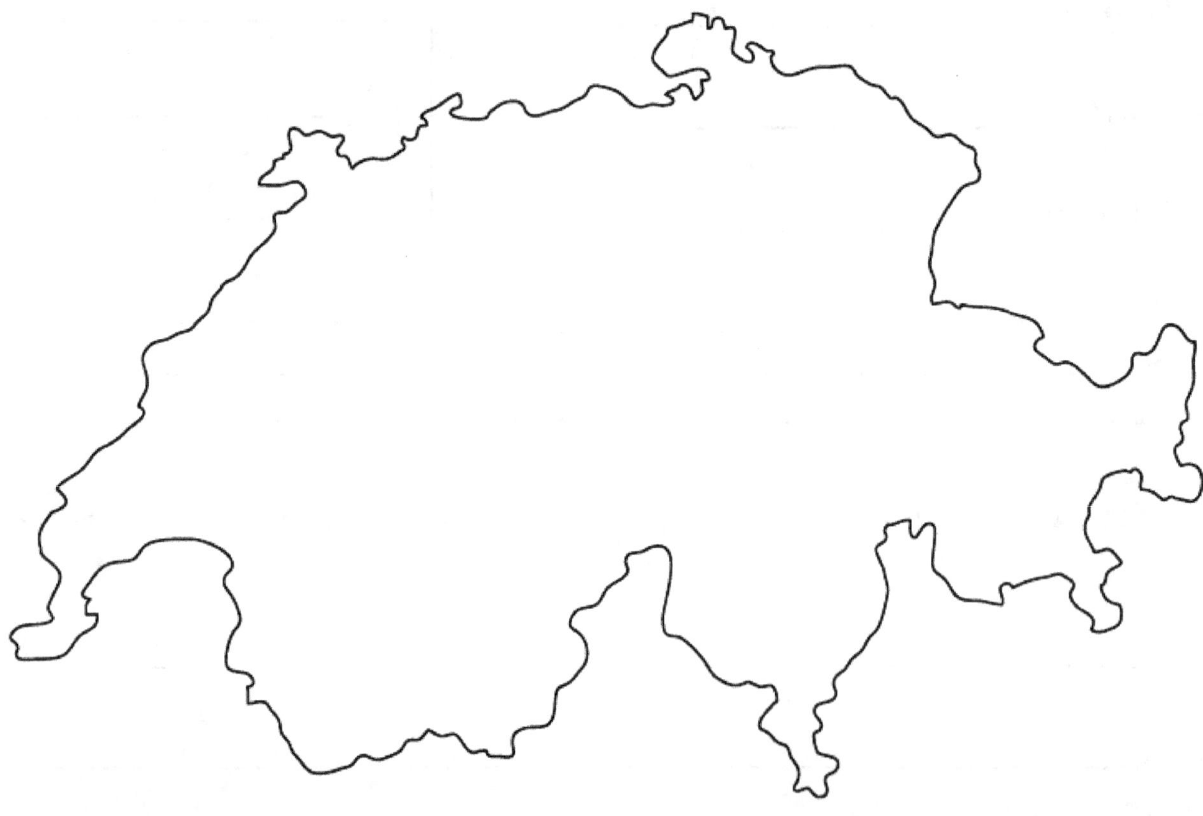

Label the capital city and any major physical features such as mountains, rivers, oceans or seas **in or around** this country.

Country Name: Switzerland

Population:____________________

Area: ____________________

Type of Government: ____________

Capital City: __________________

Religion(s): __________________

Language(s): __________________

Currency: ____________________

Climate: ____________________

Time Zone: ____________________

Major Exports

1:________________

2: ________________

3: ________________

Mountains, Rivers and Lakes

1:________________

2: ________________

3: ________________

Other Cool Things about this Country

1:____

2: ____

3: ____

4: ____

Ukraine

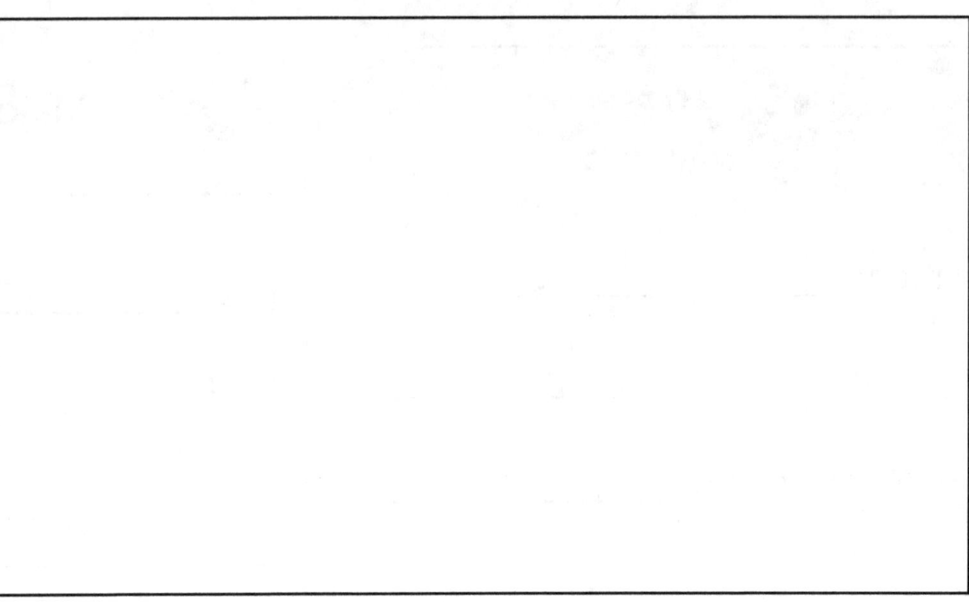

Color the country's flag in the box above.

Label the capital city and any major physical features such as mountains, rivers, oceans or seas **in or around** this country.

Country Name: Ukraine

Population: ____________________

Area: ____________________

Type of Government: ____________________

Capital City: ____________________

Religion(s): ____________________

Language(s): ____________________

Currency: ____________________

Climate: ____________________

Time Zone: ____________________

Major Exports

1: ____________________

2: ____________________

3: ____________________

Mountains, Rivers and Lakes

1: ____________________

2: ____________________

3: ____________________

Other Cool Things about this Country

1: ____________________

2: ____________________

3: ____________________

4: ____________________

United Kingdom

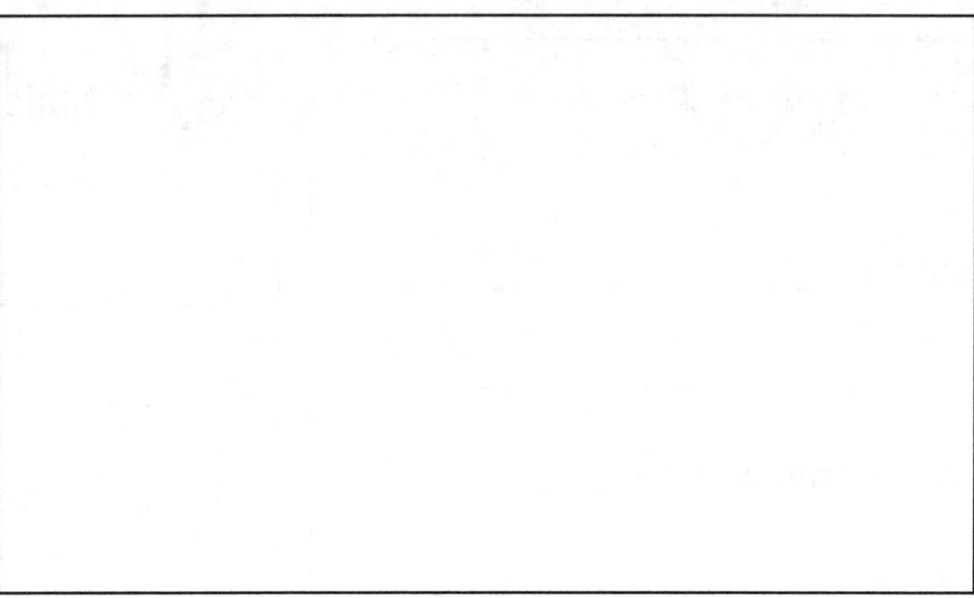

Color the country's flag in the box above.

Label the capital city and any major physical features such as mountains, rivers, oceans or seas **in or around** this country.

Country Name: United Kingdom

Population:________________________

Area: ____________________________

Type of Government: _______________

Capital City: ______________________

Religion(s): _______________________

Language(s): ______________________

Currency: _________________________

Climate: __________________________

Time Zone: ________________________

Major Exports

1:____________________

2: ____________________

3: ____________________

Mountains, Rivers and Lakes

1:______________________

2: _____________________

3: _____________________

Other Cool Things about this Country

1:____

2: ____

3: ____

4: ____

About Exploring Expression

My name is Brandy Champeau

I am an author, speaker and curriculum developer. Through my company, Exploring Expression, I help parents, caregivers and educators of K12 students become the very best expression of themselves so that they can make learning fun, easy and natural not just for their children, but for themselves as well.

At Exploring Expression, we focus on 4 specific offerings:

1. We build quality learning resources for K12 students
2. We create resources for parents and educators to help them become the best expressions of themselves and equip them to better facilitate learning opportunities for their children
3. We utilize public speaking platforms to spread the message of becoming the best expression of yourself through the cultivation of a learning lifestyle
4. We help people with a message find their voice, publish their books and create curriculum or training to share with the world

As you can see, our passion is learning - learning about yourself and learning about the world. We focus on self-improvement and education. Because in the end it all comes down to learning. Learning doesn't have to be hard and it doesn't have to be boring. At Exploring Expression we want to help you put the engagement and excitement back into education and to put the education back into life.

Connect With Us

We would love to hear from you!

https://ExploringExpression.com

ExploringExpression@gmail.com

https://www.facebook.com/ExploringExpression

https://www.Instagram.com/ExploringExpression

https://www.twitter.com/ExExAdmin

http://www.Pinterest.com/ExploringExpression

https://bit.ly/2KZrSFG

Collect all 5 Geography Factbooks!!

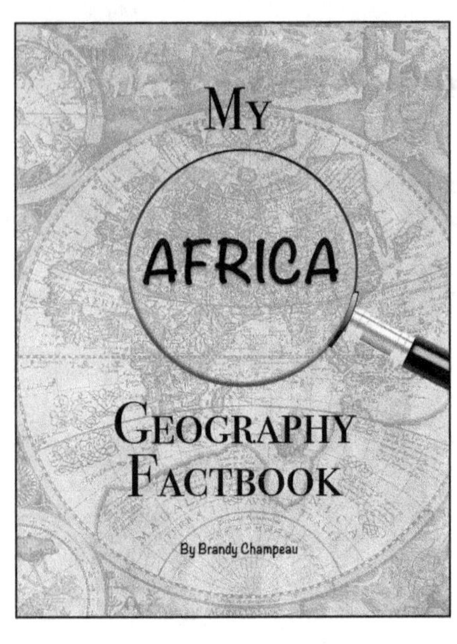

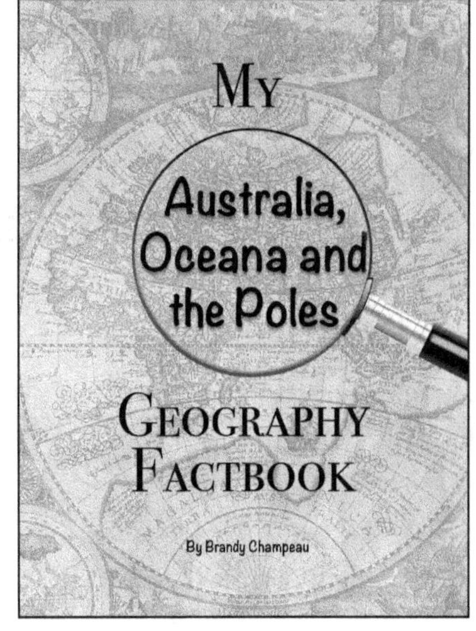

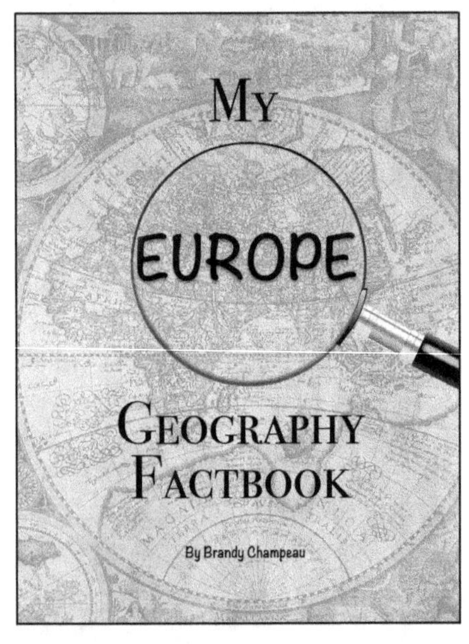

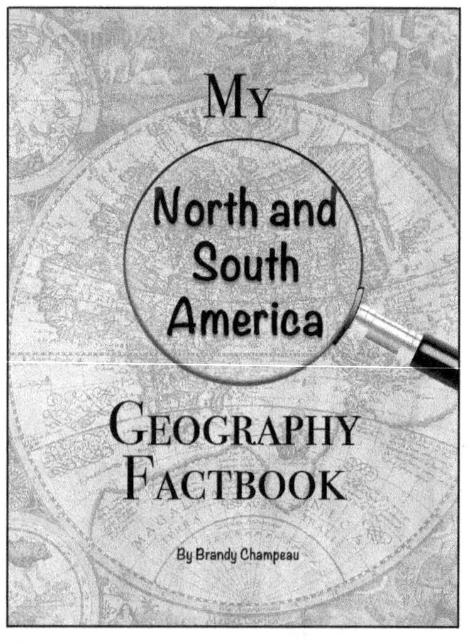

Available Now at https://ExploringExpression.com or on Amazon!!

Introducing Celebrating Today

These books are half journal, half information, and all fun.

Everyday is worth celebrating. It doesn't matter if it is a bad day, a good day or a boring day. It's still worth celebrating simply because you still have today. Every day is a new opportunity for greatness and living your best expression.

So Let's start celebrating - Today!

Available Now at https://ExploringExpression.com or on Amazon!!

Also by Brandy Champeau

Check out these Children's Books and Workbooks by Brandy Champeau.

Available at ExploringExpression.com or on Amazon

www.ingramcontent.com/pod-product-compliance
Lightning Source LLC
LaVergne TN
LVHW080322110826
845155LV00026B/181